Wilson's Raid

WILSON'S RAID

The Final Blow to the Confederacy

RUSSELL W. BLOUNT JR.

THE History PRESS

Published by The History Press
Charleston, SC
www.historypress.net

First published 2018

Manufactured in the United States

ISBN 9781467139038

Library of Congress Control Number: 2017958379

For Bob and Cheryl.

Beat! beat! drums!—blow! bugles! blow!
Through the windows—through doors—burst like a ruthless force,
Into the solemn church, and scatter the congregation.
Into the school where the scholar is studying;
Leave not the bridegroom quiet—no happiness must he have now with his bride.
Nor the peaceful farmer any peace, ploughing his field or gathering his grain.
So fierce you whirr and pound you drums—so shrill you bugles blow.

Beat! Beat! Drums!

—from "Drum Taps," Walt Whitman, 1865

Contents

Preface

Even with the most vivid of imaginations it's hard to visualize the largest body of cavalry ever assembled on the American continent moving deep into enemy-occupied territory with the speed and audacity of Wilson's Raiders in their expedition of 1865. Yet that is precisely what happened in the closing months of the American Civil War, as James Harrison Wilson led 13,480 Union horsemen on a rampage through the heart of Dixie, a land that until then had hardly been touched by the ravages of war yet held the South's industrial production centers so vital to the Confederacy's war effort. To reach and destroy those all-important targets, the raiders traveled a distance of 525 miles through an inhospitable land. Much of it, though rich in iron, was a hilly, barren region, covered with forests of pine and oak, unsuitable for subsistence and inhabited by some of the South's poorest and most impoverished people. But in the middle of it all was another land, a genteel one, embracing Alabama's Black Belt, where huge plantations sprawled across the rich alluvial soil left by the rivers, producing vast, shimmering fields of cotton from slave labor.

In this book I have attempted to take the reader on a wartime journey through this land. Along the way, into and out of such towns as Tuscaloosa, Selma and Montgomery, many characters will be introduced—soldiers, civilians, men and women—most of them being just ordinary people experiencing the ferocity of war. Others, though, will need no introduction. They are the politicians, like Jefferson Davis, and generals, such as Ulysses S. Grant, who have made their place in history by a combination of destiny and fate. But all of them, through their letters, eyewitness accounts and journals, tell this story of mounted warfare that destroyed the last of the Confederacy's infrastructure along with any shred of hope remaining with its people and their dying cause.

At the time Wilson completed his raid, Americans paid little attention to what many historians have since considered to be the greatest cavalry expedition of the war and the single most important accomplishment of Wilson's career. There were, of course, reasons for this. First, the expedition ended about the same time the war did. So even though Selma, the South's vital ordnance manufacturing center, and Montgomery, the symbolic cradle of the Confederacy, were taken, the raid did not, in the final analysis, achieve strategic success in ending the war. What's more, it was lost in the shadows of Lee's surrender to Grant and Johnston's surrender to Sherman. Those events, along with the assassination of President Lincoln, dominated the headlines. Finally, because the raid was so dangerous, journalists were forbidden to accompany the fast-moving horsemen. Thus, without newspaper coverage, it received little of the fame associated with other successful campaigns. The sole exception came shortly after the raid, when Wilson's cavalrymen captured Confederate president Jefferson Davis, a feat that instantly attracted the nation's attention.

In telling the story of Wilson's Raid, this book centers on two fascinating characters: Wilson, of course, and the man who stood in his path of destruction, Nathan Bedford Forrest. At only twenty-seven years old, Wilson was referred to as the "Boy General" by his colleagues. Brash, opinionated and brimming with confidence, Wilson was a favorite of Ulysses Grant, who considered him to be one of the army's most talented young officers and a man who could get things done. And it was with Grant's support and blessing that Wilson was given permission to lead his horsemen on an independent expedition through the Deep South, proving the young general's belief that cavalry, moving fast and striking hard, could be more effective than infantry in realizing victory.

His rival combatant was the legendary Nathan Bedford Forrest, a formidable opponent by any measure. Semiliterate and without any formal education, military or otherwise, he had a brilliant genius for warfare, and to this day many consider him the greatest cavalry commander who ever lived. After all, no soldier on either side ascended through the ranks from private to lieutenant general, except Forrest. In better times, he was brilliantly successful in victory after victory, but by 1865, circumstances had changed. In this last campaign, he was operating at a great disadvantage. Four years of constant fighting had nearly destroyed his once-great veteran cavalry. The few who remained were joined by conscripts who were mostly young boys and old men, and they were hopelessly outnumbered as they tried to stop Wilson's mounted invasion.

Although this book is clearly not intended to be a biography of Forrest, here it seems only appropriate to say a few words about the man himself. In recent years, Forrest has been a controversial, often derided subject. Indeed, given his character and record, Forrest was bound to attract critics. Many are outraged by his very existence and scornfully cast him as nothing but a slave trader—brutal, bloodthirsty and racist, bent on fighting a reactionary war to preserve white supremacy. And in some measure, those charges are undeniable. But with Forrest, as with any historical character, I think that hindsight should be employed with discretion. In other words, it's hardly appropriate to judge a man's beliefs on the issues of his day by the ideological standards of our time. Forrest was born and raised in frontier America, a land where differences were settled with a pistol and slavery was the accepted norm. To survive in that world, he was naturally driven by his times, and violence seemed to be an expected, even moral reaction, as he perceived and understood it. Placing him in his proper context, in the light of his time, I'm sure the reader will agree that for whatever else he may have been, Forrest was an exceptional, if not remarkable, man.

In this last campaign of the war, the forty-four-year-old "Wizard of the Saddle" was, for the first time, forced to come to grips with the fact that he was beaten. And he admitted this to Wilson shortly after the battle for Selma. This does not mean that Wilson was a better general than Forrest. Hardly. But because Selma was so vital to the Confederacy and was defended by Forrest, its champion cavalry commander, Wilson's victory there took on a special luster of historical importance—so important, in fact, that Union general C.C. Andrews, writing after the war, remarked, "The capture of Selma must be regarded as the most remarkable achievement in the history of modern cavalry."

Those, then, are some of my motivations and reasons for attempting to write this book. For the readers who are primarily interested in the military operations of Wilson and Forrest in this last campaign, I trust they will not be disappointed. The story includes vivid descriptions of marches through difficult country, incidents along the way and the combat of the skirmishes and battles. For readers who are simply curious about civilian life in Alabama during the Civil War, there are a number of primary accounts of people voicing their attitudes and concerns about the war in general and, more particularly, about the conduct of the soldiers during the turbulent occupations of their cities and towns. Thanks to those accounts, taken from letters, diaries and journals, we can have an intimate look at not only their personal experiences but also their characters, all of which I hope the reader will find well worth knowing. As in my previous books, I've attempted to place the reader in the context of the times rather than experiencing the story through historical hindsight. So, apart from background, recollection and analytical passages, the book is written in the present tense. I'm hopeful the reader will enjoy approaching the story in this style.

Needless to say, none of this could have been accomplished without the help of others. And here I would like to offer my thanks to those who have given me assistance in writing this book. As with any history that has been as well documented as the American Civil War, there have been some very good historians who have already chronicled this event. Specifically, I would like to thank James Pickett Jones and Noah Andre Trudeau for their work and extensive research on Wilson's Raid, a Civil War campaign that has oftentimes been ignored or neglected by others. There are, of course, many other scholars who have made contributions to particular areas of interest relative to the campaign that are contained in books, historical quarterlies and other secondary sources. Regrettably, those are too numerous to list, but Edward G. Longacre, Alston Fitts III, John Kent Folmar and Scott W. Owens are just a few who come to mind.

Much of the time devoted to the book was, as usual, spent in libraries and historical archives. Thankfully, there are many helpful folks within the walls of such places. In the Local History and Genealogy Division of the Mobile Public Library, I owe a debt of gratitude to Janie Daugherty, Roy Tucker and manager Valerie Ellis for their help in providing me access to many indispensable sources, such as the 128-volume collection of the U.S. government's *Official Records* relating to the war, known simply as the *OR* to those of us who spend our time wading through it. Another valuable repository in my research was the Alabama Department of Archives and History in Montgomery. My visit there was not only productive but enjoyable as well. Many thanks go to Nancy Dupree, Scotty Kirkland and Ken Barr for providing valuable assistance in researching newspapers, unpublished letters, diaries and other primary material contained there.

While attempting to collect information and material for this book, a number of others along the way have kindly made contributions and deserve special praise. Again, from the Alabama Department of Archives and History, Meredith McDonough provided a number of rare photographs, many of which I had believed to be unattainable. Geoff Hunt, Amie Oliver and Kathy Hinton from Baylor University and Thomas Boucher, archivist with the University of Alabama, were all helpful in locating illustrations and long-forgotten photographs. For the excellent maps of Wilson's Raid and the Battle of Selma, I owe a debt of gratitude to John Sipperly, the cartographer who prepared them. To author and historian John Sledge, a word of thanks is needed for guiding me in locating some important primary sources. Thanks also to Mr. Walter Dockery from Tuscaloosa, who furnished a compilation of essays edited by Matthew Clinton entitled *The Federal Invasion of Tuscaloosa, 1865*, which included some very interesting eyewitness accounts of that event.

And, of course, I would like to express my everlasting appreciation to the editorial board of The History Press in Mount Pleasant, South Carolina, for agreeing to publish this book. Editors Amanda Irle and Ryan Finn provided excellent editorial guidance and advice, along with a generous amount of kindness and patience. For Amanda, Ryan and the entire staff at The History Press, I am profoundly grateful for their efforts in making this a good book.

Finally, but first in my heart, I owe my family a great debt of gratitude, one I can never repay. Here, words like *gratitude*, *appreciate* and *thanks* seem pathetically inadequate. In many ways, this book was a family project. My wife, Elaine Hartley Blount, served in every role from proofreader to researcher, director of technology and my biggest fan. And my son, Russell W. Blount III, affectionately known to me as Trip, worked tirelessly with the maps, rare photographs and permissions and was an enthusiastic collaborator. To them go my sincere thanks and love.

Chapter 1

Boots and Saddles

Late on a Saturday night, February 23, 1865, a meeting begins in the living room of a crude frame house near the railroad town of West Point, Mississippi. The meeting is unusual for a number of reasons, not the least of which is the fact that the attendees are enemies, embroiled in the waning days of the American Civil War. Present is a group of army officers dressed in both the blue and gray uniforms of the Union and Confederate armies, along with one man in civilian clothing. For the past two days, the Union party, consisting of a few officers and a cavalry escort, totaling about twenty men and led by Colonel John G. Parkhurst, has traveled by horseback under a flag of truce from the Tennessee River to this point. After miles in the saddle, they arrive at about 9:00 p.m. on a moonless night that is cold and laced with a drizzling rain. Wet, chilled and tired, the officers shed their ponchos and enter the small house, which is lit only by the soft glow of candlelight. They are greeted by a dignified civilian, Judge Robert L. Caruthers, the exiled governor-elect of the state of Tennessee, as well as two soldiers in gray. One is the legendary Lieutenant General Nathan Bedford Forrest, and the other is his assistant adjutant, Major Charles W. Anderson.[1]

Ostensibly, the purpose for this meeting is to discuss an exchange of prisoners between the two sides. Only the week before, Union general George H. Thomas, commanding the Department of the Tennessee, decided to act on this matter and ordered his provost marshal, Colonel Parkhurst, to go and try to negotiate an exchange with the Confederate authorities. However, if that should prove impossible, Parkhurst should at least seek permission to deliver a supply of shoes, clothing and blankets to the seven thousand Federal soldiers being held prisoner by Forrest in Mississippi. There are, however, other reasons for this meeting—reasons not so apparent to everyone but known by a young captain who is traveling with the party.[2]

The captain is Lewis M. Hosea, a recent West Point graduate, who has been ordered to go along with Parkhurst to help him with the exchange, as well as to "incidentally" engage in some clandestine duty. His orders, however, did not come from Thomas, but from a twenty-seven-year-old general named James H. Wilson, called the "Boy General" by some, but one of Ulysses S. Grant's most favored and trusted cavalry commanders. Wilson now serves as commander of cavalry in the west and is the man who, at this moment, is busy organizing and outfitting the largest cavalry force ever assembled on the North American continent—a force that will drive into the heartland of the Confederacy, defeat the Rebels and destroy their munitions factories along with everything of military importance in its path. "Wilson's Raid," as it will come to be known, will be another part of Grant's grand plan to finish the South once and for all and will occur in conjunction with William Sherman's march across Georgia and the Carolinas and Edward R.S. Canby's campaign against Mobile, Alabama. It will, Grant believes, be a vitally important contribution toward ending the war.

In preparing for this, Wilson must gather all the information he can on the strength and plans of his adversary, Nathan Bedford Forrest, who is now defending Alabama and Mississippi. And to accomplish this, Hosea's presence at the meeting is a necessity. Wilson values Hosea as "one of my most intelligent officers" and knows he will "keep his eyes open." While Parkhurst is occupied negotiating the exchange of prisoners, Wilson wants Hosea to concentrate on Forrest, telling him "to interview that wily commander, to study his frame of mind, and to gather such information as he could get in regard to the country, its food supplies and military resources…no precaution should be neglected and no information left unsought."[3]

As the meeting drags on through the night, Hosea stares through the flickering light of the burning candles, studying the man across the table. He needs to know what kind of man this could be—a man whom no Union general has been able to defeat and a man known for his terrible, homicidal wrath and feared by friend and foe alike. Some even wonder whether he is a man at all. "A devil," Sherman calls him, claiming he must be "hunted down and killed if it cost ten thousand lives and bankrupts the Federal Treasury." But Hosea's impressions of the general, written in a letter home following the meeting, hardly seem demonic and are even flattering:

> *The general effect* [of Forrest] *is suggestive of notables of Revolutionary times, with powdered hair as we see them in portraits of that day; and to our unaccustomed eyes the rich gray uniform with its embroidered collar added much to the effect produced. His habitual expression seemed rather subdued and thoughtful, but when his face lighted up with a smile, which ripples all over his features, the effect is really charming…His language indicates a very limited education, but his impressive manner conceals many otherwise notable defects.*

So goes Hosea's first impressions of Bedford Forrest. His trailing remark about "notable defects" is apparently in reference to the continuous grammatical errors in Forrest's speech, but then he adds, "In a very short time, however, these pass unnoticed."[4]

The meeting, which drags on until four o'clock in the morning, produces only limited progress in terms of the prisoner exchange. Although Forrest does not object to the exchange, he prefers to confer with his superior, Lieutenant General Richard Taylor, commanding the Confederate Department of Alabama and Mississippi, before any final arrangements can be made. During the course of the night-long meeting, however, the conversation reveals much to Captain Hosea about the Rebel general but, as expected, very little of his "numbers and plans." Later, as Hosea is relating to the "Boy General" the results of the meeting and his impressions of Forrest, it became apparent to Wilson that Forrest, too, had succeeded in gathering some information about him. "He seemed curious to learn what he could about me and my career," remembers Wilson.[5]

Before the meeting, Forrest knew nothing of Wilson, except that it was his Union cavalrymen he was fighting in Tennessee while covering Hood's retreat after the disastrous campaign at Nashville. During the meeting, according to Wilson's account, Hosea tells Forrest "that I [Wilson] was a West Pointer, an officer of engineers, had recently commanded a division of Philip Sheridan's cavalry, and had some knowledge of tactics, strategy and military organization." Forrest, apparently not impressed by the well-educated young man, responds to Wilson's credentials by telling Hosea that he knows "nothing of military tactics, except what he had learned in actual campaigning." Then, as an afterthought, he adds here the words he's most remembered for: "But I always make it a rule to get there first with the most men"—still a fundamental principle of warfare valued by military men to this day.[6]

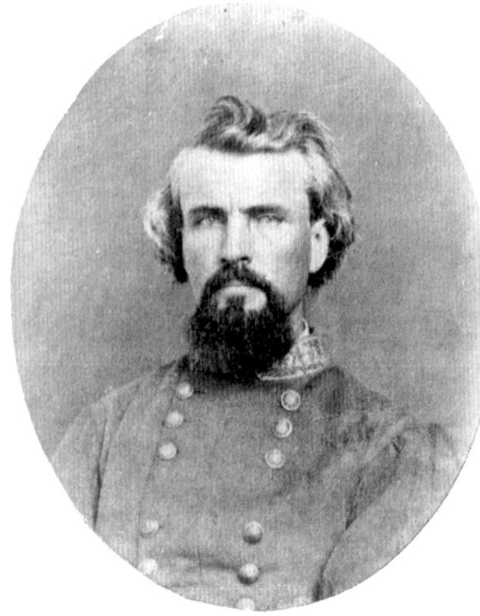

Confederate general Nathan Bedford Forrest, commanding all Confederate cavalry forces in Mississippi and Alabama. *Courtesy Library of Congress.*

Forrest talks on through the night on a number of subjects, including guerrillas, who claim to be soldiers but, for the most part, are just criminals or deserters, marauding through the countryside and terrorizing civilians. He is sincere and adamant when he tells Parkhurst that he's "as anxious to rid the country of guerillas as any officer in the U.S. Army, and that he would deem it a favor if General Thomas would hang every one caught." The pugnacious Forrest, though, always returns to his favorite subject of fighting, comparing his methods of warfare to those of "old school soldiers." Captain Hosea listens quietly while Forrest gratuitously shares his own views of how cavalrymen should fight, declaring his preference for six-shooters over sabers. "I don't want nary [a] saber in my command—haven't got one."[7]

It has now become obvious to Hosea that all of Forrest's bravado is meant to reach the ears of James Wilson, who Forrest realizes will be his next opponent. Hosea, Forrest knows, will return to the man who sent him, telling him every word that has been spoken here, and the Rebel general wants Wilson to understand that he considers this visit a challenge. And so, as Hosea is leaving the meeting, Forrest tells him, "Captain, you can tell General Wilson that I have picked out a first rate place for a cavalry battle down here and if he'll come down with any force he pleases, I'll meet him with the same number and agree to whip the fight."[8]

The next day, Forrest travels to Meridian, Mississippi, to meet with Richard Taylor and get his final approval for the exchange of prisoners. While he's away, the Parkhurst party waits in the small town of Rienzi, Mississippi, for some definite word from Forrest on when and where the exchange will occur. The approval comes a few days later, but so does a downpour of rain, swelling the rivers, washing out roads and stranding Parkhurst and his men for another week in Rienzi. During this time, young Captain Hosea passes the time writing letters home and sending reports to Wilson about what he has learned. Finally, the rain slackens and the waters subside long enough for them to begin the trip back to rejoin their army. Before leaving, however, Hosea, still thinking about encountering the famous Forrest, goes to the telegraph office and sends a wire to Judge Robert Caruthers, the civilian who was present at the meeting. Knowing the judge to be a very educated man, and one who would appreciate the classics, he sends the telegram in Latin: *Haec olim meminisse juvabit tetegisse dextrano tyranni*, taken from Virgil's epic poem, the *Aeneid*, and translated, "Hereafter it will rejoice me to remember that I have touched the right hand of your leader."[9]

On the same day the meeting with Forrest is taking place, James Wilson is conducting a grand review of his cavalry corps at Gravelly Springs, Alabama, mostly for the benefit of George Thomas, his immediate superior. As three divisions of mounted men pass in formation, the burly Thomas is clearly impressed with what he sees. Riding past him are row after row of horse soldiers, gently swaying in their McClellan saddles, smartly dressed in light-blue trousers accented with a yellow stripe and dark-blue jackets, topped with a forage cap and each armed with a Spencer repeating carbine, a six-shot Colt revolver and a polished cavalry saber. Accompanying each division is a battery of artillery, consisting of four twelve-pound Napoleons. Indeed, it's a handsome display of well-drilled soldiers, wielding the most superior weapons and equipment of the time.[10]

For Grant, Sherman and Thomas, the original plan for Wilson's cavalry corps was to move through Alabama and demonstrate against the Confederate cities of Tuscaloosa, Montgomery and the all-important city of Selma, containing the vital munition industries that have been sustaining the Southern war effort. However, the Union brass had, until now, only envisioned Wilson's campaign as diversionary one that would distract the enemy's attention away from Canby, whom Grant has ordered to take Mobile with his large army and then to push northward, destroying Selma, Montgomery and whatever else stood in his path. Wilson, though, is disappointed and unhappy with this minor role in the campaign and has continued to doggedly press Grant and Thomas to allow him to make a full-scale invasion using his entire mounted force. He wants to work independently without Canby's help and with his own forces will take and destroy everything of military value in Tuscaloosa, Montgomery and Selma.

Almost immediately after Thomas finishes witnessing the grand cavalry review, he listens again to Wilson's aggressive plan and considers what an awesome blow this could deliver to the enemy, and his mind is suddenly changed. "From that moment," recalls Wilson, "[I] had his entire support and confidence." The young general is then instructed by Thomas to "get his command in readiness for just such a campaign…and to capture those places if possible, after accomplishing which, he was to operate against any of the enemy's forces in the direction of Mississippi, Mobile, or Macon, as circumstances might demand." Only days later, Thomas's new orders for Wilson are approved by Grant, who also blesses the young cavalry general with the authority to "pursue such a course as [Wilson] might see proper, keeping in view the general objects of the impending campaign." In other words, Grant has given Wilson what he's always wanted: "The amplest discretion as an independent commander."[11]

James Harrison Wilson is elated with what he believes is a well-deserved opportunity to be a main character in this war and establish his place in history. After all, as one biographer describes him, "[He] was a brash and impatient young man who had a lofty opinion of his own capabilities." But those capabilities should have been a source of pride for him. Wilson, in fact, is a man of exceptional motivation, strong opinions and great will power and is possessed with a clever military mind. Unfortunately, his admirable characteristics are, at times, overshadowed by an autocratic and conceited personality. Nevertheless, nearly all of his fellow officers and superiors admit that "Harry" Wilson, as he's sometimes called, is a brilliant young officer.[12]

Born in 1837 on his father's farm near Shawneetown, Illinois, Wilson was forced from an early age to mature quickly and accept the awesome responsibility of providing for his family. His father, Harrison, died in 1852, leaving James, who was only fourteen, as the oldest male in the home. In the enterprising role of the family breadwinner, he was so successful that he developed somewhat of an exaggerated confidence that he could handle any situation or problem life might hand him. A few years later, that confidence proved valuable when he received an appointment to the military academy at West Point. Wilson's class numbered 121 cadets when he enrolled, but as they faced the rigorous academic schedule and draconian discipline, they began to slowly drop out or to be dismissed until two-thirds of them were gone. But not Wilson. Assured by his sharp mind and fueled by determination and driving ambition, he graduated in 1860, finishing 6th out of the 41 cadets who managed to complete the program.

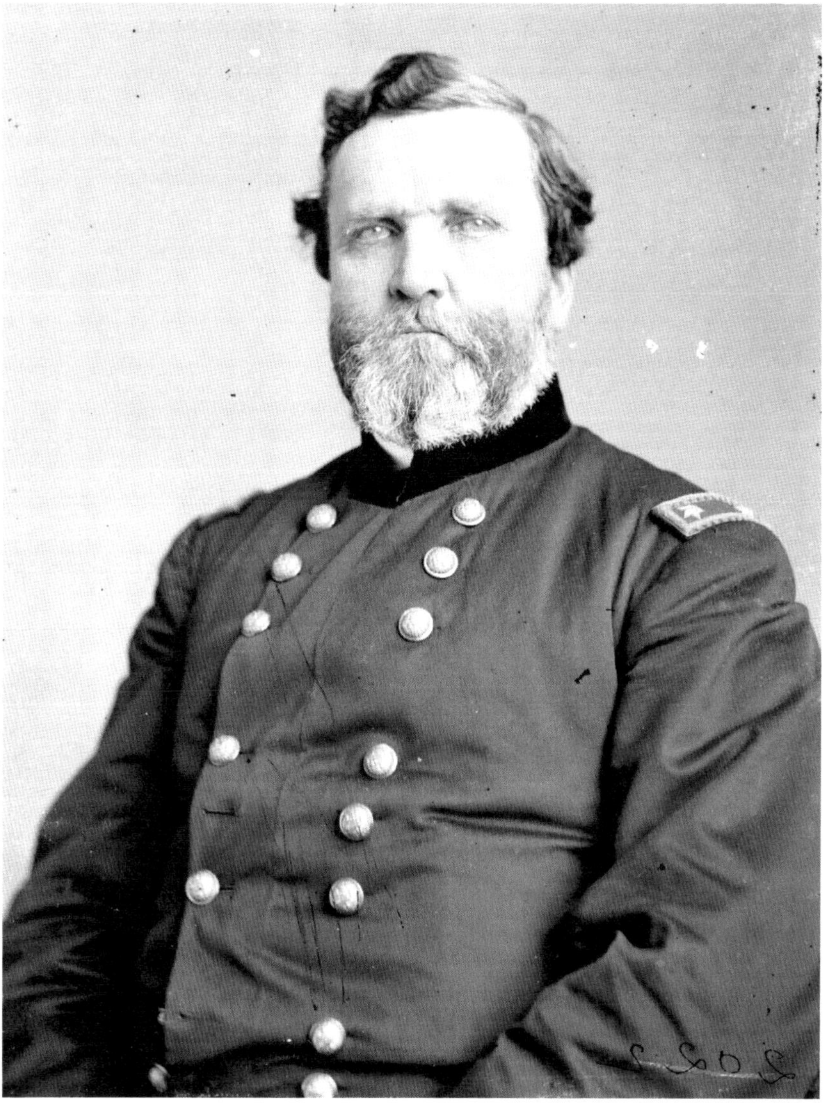

Union general George H. Thomas, Federal commander of the Department of Tennessee. *Courtesy Library of Congress.*

Not long after graduation, Wilson finds himself in the middle of a great civil war. For the first three years of the conflict, he proves himself time and again to be a dependable soldier of unbridled energy and resourcefulness. Smart and well grounded in the science of military tactics, he continues to excel in one campaign after another. Physically, though, Wilson is not especially impressive. Standing about five feet, ten inches tall with a slender build, he's described as "a slight person of a light complexion and with a rather pinched face." But there is nothing ordinary about his determined and energetic character. Some of his fellow officers, however, find him to be outspoken, conceited, arrogant, domineering and completely devoid of humor. Nevertheless, his reputation as an excellent cavalry commander continues to grow until he is finally promoted to brigadier, making him the youngest general in the service. Having strong opinions and a tendency to alienate others does not seem to be much of a detriment in his rise through the ranks. This is probably due to the fact that even though Wilson is, at times, critical of some of his superiors, he is smart enough to keep his opinions private, airing them only in letters to his closest friends. And those letters are, of course, a tribute to his literary abilities. Undeniably, he is an excellent writer, as evidenced by his wartime reports, letters and memorandums, not to mention the well-written autobiography he will produce later in life. He's also a voracious reader and lover of books, always keeping a few with him, even during those days he spends in the saddle. In short, Wilson is a man of many parts, most of which are admirable and go to make up a successful young general who will soon lead the largest cavalry expedition of the war.[13]

Although Wilson is anxious to begin his campaign, which was expected to get underway early in March, the rains continue to pour day after day, leaving the roads impassable with mud and swelling the rivers beyond their banks. "I am greatly provoked at the delay," complains Wilson, "but am powerless to help it." He is especially concerned that Grant would not understand the delay. Always on his mind is the memory of Grant's impatience with Thomas's delays during the Nashville Campaign. Even though the brutal winter weather had crippled the movement of the Union army and justified the delay, Thomas nearly lost his job because of it. "Isn't it unfortunate that the rain cannot be controlled by General Grant?" muses Wilson, a man usually considered too serious to indulge in any kind of humor.[14]

As the tedious, rain-filled days drag by, Wilson is becoming uneasy over the delay and what his superiors—especially Grant, whose opinion he values—might interpret as a poor performance on his part. He's never been a man who cared to accept responsibility when things went wrong, and he certainly doesn't want to start taking the blame for the weather. But he continues to fret over his dilemma. While he waits and worries, there are frequent letters exchanged between Wilson and several members of the staff at Grant's headquarters. In one from Wilson to Adam Badeau, Grant's military secretary, he writes apologetically, "I am sorry your letters

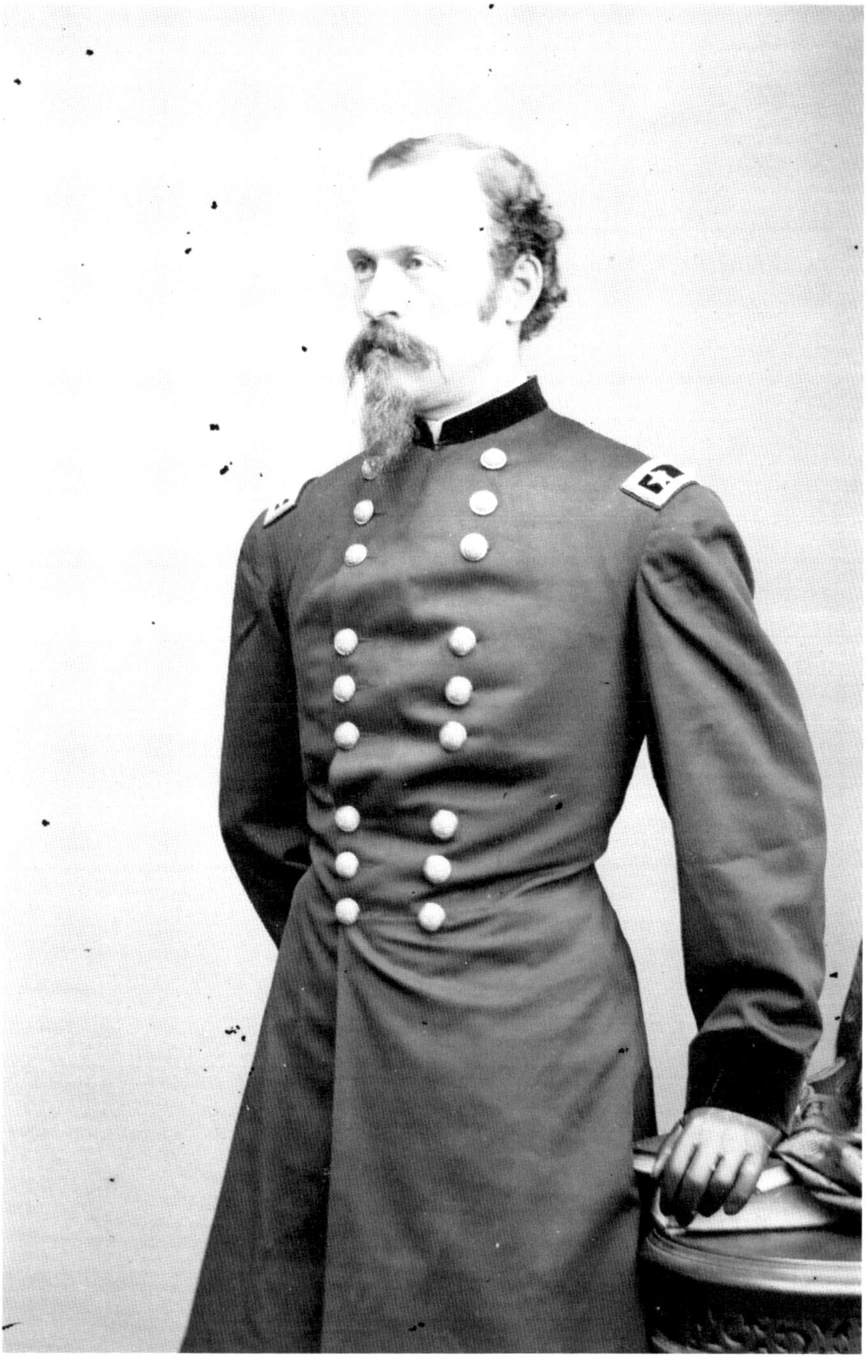

Union general James Harrison Wilson, the "Boy General," commander of all the Federal cavalry in the western theater. *Courtesy Library of Congress.*

find me here instead of on the road to Dixie as the General expects and as I hoped. This is the only time in my life I was ever ordered to start by a certain date and could not do it....The Tennessee [River] is higher than ever before known...but I venture to hope the General will not lose any of his confidence in my promptitude and determination."[15]

Wilson is sure, however, that no one can fault him for a lack of preparation and training. Since January, he has been putting his cavalrymen through training programs, drills, inspections and exercises in discipline to the point where his corps is an efficient fighting force. Beyond the training, he has made certain the three divisions he intends to make the trip are all mounted, well armed and supplied. Nearly his entire corps is furnished with the repeating Spencer rifles and six-shot revolvers. Commissary rations, ammunition, horseshoes, medical supplies and other provisions have all been stockpiled, ready to load onto 250 wagons. There is also the matter of fording the many streams and rivers in his path, and for this he has organized a pontoon train consisting of fifty-six mule wagons containing enough boats to construct a four-hundred-foot bridge "My command is certainly in magnificent condition," brags Wilson, "well armed, splendidly mounted, perfectly clad and equipped, and will turn out a heavier fighting force than ever before on a similar expedition in this country."[16]

After so much preparation and planning, everyone is anxious and ready to move. But the rains continue, along with the bitter cold of one of the most severe winters on record. Restless men curl up in their tents waiting for a break in the weather. As expected, many of them become sick in such miserable conditions and begin crowding the camp hospitals. Then, if the situation wasn't distressful enough, the Tennessee River spills over its banks, destroying "a large quantity of grain accumulated for the horses" and washing away a number of supply wagons. Flash floods inundate the camps and water streams through the tents. Soldiers are forced to rush frantically around the camps, moving their belongings and supplies to higher ground. Morale plummets as some of the men begin to lose their enthusiasm, and everyone curses the weather.[17]

By March 12, the rains have slackened, and the Tennessee River begins to rapidly fall to a more normal stage. The next day, Wilson issues orders for the troops to begin moving toward the landings on the north bank, causing the cavalrymen's spirits to soar when they hear the news. By March 15, the first of Wilson's horse soldiers have been transported across the river. During the next three days, the entire corps is ferried over to the south bank, where it goes into camp and waits for its supply wagons and animal forage to arrive.

"I hope we shall be off in time to do good service," writes Wilson, as he sees things finally coming together for their departure. Then he adds with confidence, "I am personally in the best of health and spirits." So, too, are his men, as they stir from their sleep well before sunrise on March 22, 1865. After breakfast and the routine morning preparations, the bugle call, "Boots and Saddles," rings through the gray streaks of dawn, and 13,480 horsemen climb on their mounts to begin the greatest cavalry adventure of the Civil War—one that will be remembered by both sides as "Wilson's Raid."[18]

Chapter 2

"First with the Most"

As Wilson prepares for his grand expedition into the heartland of the Confederacy, Southerners are facing the darkest days of the war. Their armies, once victorious, have now been battered and driven back. Most of their cities have been taken and occupied. And with every Southern port now blockaded, they suffer from severe shortages of medicine, clothing and other necessities. Confederate paper money is nearly worthless, and the economy is in shambles. Invading Union armies have laid waste to thousands of farms and plantations, leaving many people homeless, destitute and wandering from town to town in search of food and shelter. Beyond losing the battles and territory, the South's most irreplaceable loss is the flower of its manhood—soldiers, hundreds of thousands of them, killed, wounded or captured.

Considering all the death, misery and hardships enveloping their land, it's a small wonder that many Southerners have simply lost the will to go on fighting a war they consider lost. "We are literally a land of mourning," wails a South Carolina newspaper late in the war. And that sentiment is becoming more widespread throughout the Confederacy at the outset of 1865. "Look at this war," complains a Confederate officer in a letter to his wife. "It has come to everybody, states, towns, villages, families—all feel it and share in it." So it's not surprising that desertions are increasing at an alarming rate, not only from conscripts but also from volunteers who have gradually become demoralized and discouraged by so many defeats, the deaths of their comrades and the suffering and hardships that never seem to end. Still others, understandably, desert after receiving letters from their wives, complaining of hunger and desperate living conditions.[19]

There is, however, still a majority group of Southerners willing to go on fighting and sacrificing for a cause they privately fear is lost. Such determination is a result of a stubborn, perhaps even haughty pride. And as a proud people, they find the thought of losing to the Yankees, whom they consider to be immoral, ill bred and generally an inferior class of people, to be intolerable. Moreover, most Southerners are intensely religious, and even if both sides worship the same God, they cannot believe He would allow them to lose to a people they believe to be less providential than themselves. But now, in the darkest days of the war, Southerners are faced with a profound test of their Christian faith.[20]

So, as the New Year dawns on 1865, the Confederacy is gasping its last prayer. Lee's Army of Northern Virginia is stretched to the breaking point in the ditches surrounding Petersburg. It's inevitable that Grant and his huge army will soon force the collapse of the long gray line, opening the way for Richmond to be taken. In Georgia, Sherman is keeping his promise that he will make the people howl, ravaging and burning his way through the country en route to the Carolinas. And only last month, George Thomas came close to annihilating the Army of Tennessee in the hills around Nashville, leaving the ragged remnants to defend the entire western theater.

Such, then, is the South's dilemma as the Union forces prepare for a final thrust into the heart of Dixie. While Wilson's cavalry is poised to strike from North Alabama, first to Tuscaloosa and then on to Selma and Montgomery, Grant has ordered General Edward R.S. Canby to move up from Fort Morgan and Pensacola on the Gulf of Mexico with three corps of infantry and take Mobile. From there, Canby will continue north, meeting Wilson and assisting him, if necessary, in taking Selma and Montgomery. Both Wilson and Canby will have a wide latitude of discretion in their movements to achieve these goals. But Grant is not a man whose orders are to be taken lightly, and both men know he will not settle for anything less than the complete achievement of his goals.

In Meridian, Mississippi, Richard Taylor and Bedford Forrest are spending a great deal of time together in the early months of 1865, getting to know each other and trying to determine when, where and how the Union invasion of

Alabama will take place. The two men had never met prior to Taylor's appointment to command the Department of Alabama and Mississippi. The thirty-nine-year-old Taylor, son of a United States president and an 1845 graduate of Yale University, was undoubtedly curious to meet this man Forrest, a man so different from himself yet a man who, despite being a semiliterate backwoodsman, managed to rise to a legend in military circles. Thinking back on their first meeting, Taylor remembered seeing the famed cavalryman when he climbed off a train in Meridian and reported for duty: "He was a tall, stalwart man, with grayish hair, mild countenance, and slow and homely of speech."[21]

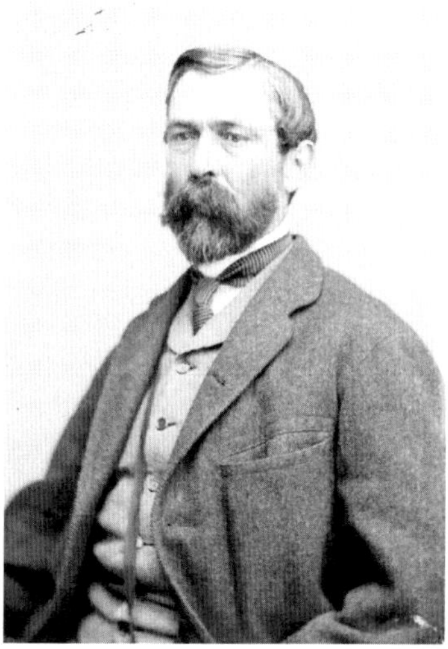

Confederate general Richard Taylor, son of President Zachary Taylor, commander of the Departments of Mississippi and Alabama. *Courtesy Library of Congress.*

In those last months of the Civil War, Taylor attempts to learn more about the character and psychology of Forrest. Like others, he has many questions. What, for example, makes him such a great commander without the benefit of a military education—or, for that matter, any formal schooling? How could even the best fighter enlist as a private and climb to the rank of lieutenant general in such a short time? What other commander has succeeded in winning nearly all his battles with inferior numbers and inferior weapons? What other commander has managed to inflict so much damage to the enemy's lines of supply and communications over so much territory? And how, too, could a man born in 1821, dirt poor in the backwoods of Tennessee, manage to amass a fortune of $1 million by the beginning of the war?[22]

It's not surprising that Taylor, for all his insight and intelligence, is not able to answer many of these questions or is not able to understand all there is to know about the man many are calling the "Wizard of the Saddle." But like Taylor, those who have served both with him and against him do understand some of the things that make him tick. They know that Forrest is a realist rather than a romantic, that he lives his life on life's terms and that he has the ability to look at a situation for what it is and to understand what must be done. What's more, his attitude toward war is unique. Causes do not motivate him as much as his private sense of duty and honor. But unlike West Point men, he reduces war to its most primitive and basic definition. "War means fighting, and fighting means killing," insists Forrest, a man who, over the years, has developed a penchant for violence—a man who fights to win. The wisdom in this simple philosophy can certainly be confirmed by many Union generals, including Abel Streight, Sooy Smith and Samuel Sturgis, all of whom have encountered him on the battlefield with disastrous results. "I doubt," admits Taylor, "if any commander since the days of lion-hearted Richard has killed as many enemies with his own hands as Forrest." Perhaps Taylor is right. Forrest has, to this point in the war, killed twenty-nine men in combat.[23]

In the heat of battle, a death-dealing rage overcomes him. His voice, normally low and quiet, turns shrill, and his face and eyes turn blood red. Watching his furious wrath in a fight makes an unforgettable impression on his troops, who welcome his very presence as having an "electric effect." A Tennessee private, having watched Forrest in battle, feels he provides an inspiration to everyone through his "terrible energy, more like that of a piece of powerful steam machinery than of a human being." No one can miss him. At six feet, two inches, he is a giant by the norms of his time. And by any standard, he is a powerfully built man of remarkable strength. Adding to such a commanding appearance are his dark gray eyes, piercing like those of a tiger and set widely over high cheek bones. His face seems almost chiseled from stone, casting a dark complexion and surrounded by iron-gray hair and a short, black Van Dyke beard.[24]

Forrest, usually depicted as a harsh soldier of violent temperament, also has other sides. "Old Bedford," it seems, can be kind and gentle, especially with women and children, in whose company he always takes great pleasure. As for religion, he does not wear it on his sleeve, which is evident by his profane cursing, but he is a Christian believer, encouraging his chaplains to hold services in camp, all of which he attends. And although humor is something that rarely occurs in his world, he does have a sense of it, as evidenced in a dinner conversation during this last campaign with a well-bred widow in Marion, Alabama. Staring at the general with curiosity, she asks him why his beard has remained black while his hair is turning gray. Forrest, searching for a dignified explanation, politely replies that he "might have used his brain a little more than he did his jaw." This is certainly an explanation that his troops believe to be true. "A massive brain," declares his chief of artillery, John W. Morton, claiming that his leader has "grasped intuitively and instantaneously the strategic possibilities of every situation which confronted him."[25]

The relationship between Forrest and the officers and men serving under his command is unique in many respects. He understands the kind of men he is dealing with precisely because he's one of them. Many of them, like Forrest, are hard-bitten backwoodsmen who were practically born on a horse with a gun in their hand. So, while he will overlook the strict military discipline and drilling practiced in other units, there are certain expectations that cannot be compromised. He insists, for example, that his officers make sure that the troops are always equipped with ammunition and weapons and the animals are well fed and cared for. In battle, the men must fight with courage and be willing to give up their lives when necessary. And whether in battle or work, he will ask nothing of them that he's not willing to do. In short, he's a man who not only directs but also takes the lead.

In return, his troops have a great respect and admiration for Forrest. There is a certain reverence, if not a total devotion, to their leader. Writing after the war, Garnet Wolseley, a British observer who has spoken with a number of these men, gives his impressions of them: "His force was largely composed of wild and reckless men, who all looked to him as their master, their leader, and over whom he had obtained the most complete control. He possessed that rare tact—unlearnable [*sic*] from books—which enabled him not only to effectively control these fiery, turbulent spirits, but to attach them to him personally with hooks of steel. In him they recognized not only the daring, able, and successful leader, but also the commanding officer who would not hesitate to punish with severity when he deemed punishment necessary." Any cowardly behavior from any of his men would certainly be cause for such punishment. He will not tolerate it. Forrest has no use and little mercy for cowards or skulkers, as he calls them. He believes in the maxim that "kindness to bad men is cruelty to the good." Punishment for a cowardly act, such as desertion, might range from a thrashing to an occasional killing. The latter, he feels, will serve as an example and gruesome reminder of what a coward might expect. Whatever punishment Forrest chooses to employ on those he judges to be "disobedient, turbulent and mutinous," he deems it "justice to those who discharge their duties with promptness and fidelity."[26]

While covering Hood's retreat after the Nashville Campaign, the men of Forrest's command had undergone their most severe test of endurance experienced during the entire war. Protecting the beaten remnants of the infantry, the rear guard fought battle after battle until the men were "ragged, barefoot [and] bloody, without food and without hope." Nevertheless, under Forrest's encouragement, they somehow kept going and maintained their morale. "We had that confidence in him which I imagine the Old Guard had in Napoleon," remembered a lieutenant in his escort. When they finally crossed the Tennessee River to safety, the ordeal was over, but the condition of the men was deplorably weak by the time they arrived in Corinth, Mississippi.[27]

Forrest now faces the almost impossible task of rebuilding his command to be an effective fighting force once again. Taylor, replacing Hood after the carnage in Tennessee, places Forrest in command of every cavalry unit in Alabama, Mississippi, West Tennessee and east Louisiana. While this may sound like an impressive sphere of authority, the truth is that this would give Forrest about ten thousand cavalrymen spread over a wide geographical area. And with this very small number, he is now expected to defend the heartland of the Confederacy. He is, of course, greatly concerned and says so in a letter to Taylor: "I will be left to defend as well as can be done this section of the country. I regret to say that the means at my disposal are not adequate to the task devolving upon me. My command is greatly reduced in numbers and efficiency by losses in battle and in the worn-down and unserviceable condition of animals." Then, almost as an afterthought, he reminds Taylor of his own condition: "I have had no rest or relief from duty since I came into this department."[28]

Forrest, though, sees little prospect for any rest in his near future. Wilson's cavalry and Canby's infantry are gathering for an invasion on both sides of him, and Sherman, as always, is clamoring for him to be "hunted down and killed." Besides, rest can come later, as he believes this may be the last campaign of the war. Privately, in a conversation with one of his officers, he admits as much: "To my mind it is evident that the end is not far off." Nevertheless, he is "honor bound" to do his duty and fight until that end comes. He knows, however, that his troops need and deserve rest and reorganization before they can face this last campaign.[29]

Urging him to order just such a rest is thirty-four-year-old James Ronald Chalmers, one of Forrest's division commanders and nominally his second in command. "I appeal to you," writes Chalmers in early January, "to save your cavalry, if possible, from a position in which they must in my judgment, certainly meet with ruin and disgrace." He goes on making a case that Forrest certainly isn't about to deny: "If we had time to reorganize, recruit, and fit up the command…we can whip the enemy's cavalry, and every man in your command is anxious that you should have a fair trial of strength with Major General Wilson."[30]

Even though Chalmers and Forrest recognize great qualities in each other, the two men have had their differences and occasional clashes of temperament. Chalmers, a Mississippi lawyer before the war, is an independent character and highly opinionated. Forrest, of course, has small use for any mortal's dissenting opinion. Having served under Forrest since 1863, Chalmers has come to know this and is now careful to guard against using any language his commander might consider to be impertinent. A case in point would be a time during the Nashville Campaign when Chalmers ordered his troops to charge into an oak thicket at what he first thought was a small cavalry outpost. Instead, it turned out to be Union infantry dug into strong fortifications. After his troops were repulsed, Forrest rode up and questioned Chalmers: "Why don't you drive those fellows off?" Chalmers then explained it was infantry he was up against. Forrest demurred: "I think you are mistaken. That's only a small cavalry force." Chalmers, fully aware that Old Bedford was not one to argue with, orders another charge into the thicket. The result was devastating. So, Chalmers and what was left of his battered horsemen again retreated and met Forrest, who had been watching the whole bloody affair. "They was in there sure enough, wasn't they Chalmers?" said Forrest. "Yes sir," replied the frustrated Chalmers, "that is the second time I found them there."[31]

Thus, it's understandable that when Chalmers ends his petition to Forrest for rest and recuperation, he adds a trailing expression of regret. "You will pardon me for the plainness of this letter, but there are times when every man should think, and not hesitate to express his thoughts." This time, however, Forrest is fully aware that Chalmers's opinion is right. In fact, orders have already been sent to Chalmers on New Year's Day that he apparently had not yet received when he made his request. Those orders directed the very action Chalmers has requested. Both men know that if Wilson is to be stopped, Forrest's cavalry will have to do it. For that to happen, there must be a period of recuperation for the men.[32]

The order from Forrest directs Chalmers to furlough most of the men from Alabama, Mississippi and Tennessee for twenty days. "Send them in charge of an officer to their homes, to collect absentees, procure clothing for those left behind, and mount themselves," writes Forrest. Then, as an added reward, he adds, "Instruct them that all men, on their return, that will bring with them a deserter or a recruit well mounted will be entitled to [another] furlough of twenty days in the next twelve months." Despite their fatigued condition, there is a "rush and hurry of that ride home." Many of the men push themselves and their horses to the limit, covering great distances in a single day, "so as not to lose an hour of precious time." After the furlough, nearly all of them return, some bringing new mounts along with men who had been absent during the last campaign because they were without horses. The time of rest has proven to be a revival of spirits and morale for the soldiers. Arriving back in camp, John Milton Hubbard, a Tennessee cavalryman, expresses his appreciation of the "fat horses, good clothes and good rations" they were finally enjoying. But he, along with every other man, also knows that the enjoyment of the holiday "would be of short duration." Keeping their promise to return during this desperate time when the number of desertions in other units is rising at an alarming rate is clearly a testament to the loyalty of the men of Forrest's command.[33]

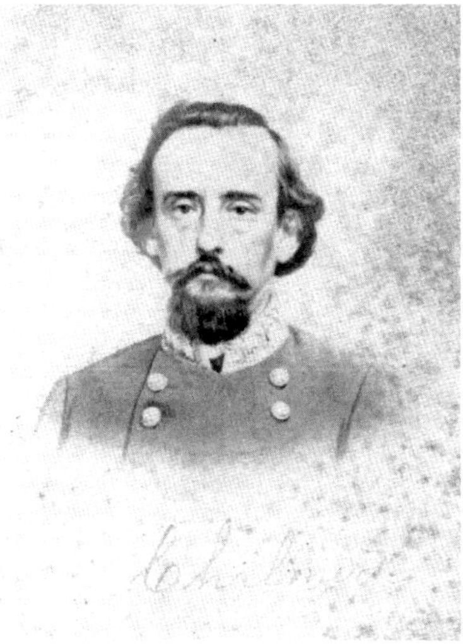

Confederate general James R. Chalmers, a division commander under Forrest. *Courtesy Alabama Department of Archives and History, Montgomery, Alabama.*

After the furlough, Forrest's next order of business is to reorganize his command. All the Mississippi troops, numbering 3,648 men, are assigned to James Chalmers, whose new division is now made up of three brigades and commanded by Frank C. Armstrong, Wirt Adams and Peter B. Starke. Thirty-year-old Frank Armstrong is a natural horse soldier. Born in the Indian Territory of Oklahoma to a father who was stationed there as a cavalry officer, Armstrong, despite his age, is a seasoned veteran, having served in many campaigns under Chalmers, Forrest and "Fighting Joe" Wheeler. Wirt Adams is also a veteran soldier and is said to have fired the last shot of the war. A rabid Mississippi secessionist, he was offered the cabinet office of postmaster general at the outset of the war but turned it down to raise and command the First Mississippi Cavalry. Peter Starke commands the remaining brigade in Chalmers's division. An older man of fifty years, he, too, is a Mississippian who had played a significant role in the defense of Vicksburg and later in the Atlanta Campaign.[34]

William H. "Red" Jackson commands another of Forrest's divisions, composed primarily of Tennesseans. Jackson himself was born and raised in Tennessee and is an 1856 graduate of West Point. His brigade commanders are Tyree H. Bell, Alexander W. Campbell and Lawrence S. Ross. Bell is a newly commissioned brigadier who has been praised by Forrest since becoming a part of his command. Like Jackson, he hails from Tennessee and has fought Yankees throughout the war. Alexander Campbell, a lawyer before the war, doesn't have a very extensive record in battle. However, this is only because he was captured in Tennessee in 1863 and has remained in a prison camp until recently, when he was exchanged and made a brigade commander under Jackson. Completing Jackson's division is the brigade commanded by Lawrence S. Ross, who is a Texan rather than a native Tennessean. Ross has a lasting reputation as a frontiersman and soldier, having fought Comanches as a Texas Ranger and then serving throughout the Civil War, enlisting as a private and eventually rising to the rank of brigadier general. Along the way, he has participated in 135 battles and has had five horses shot from under him.[35]

During this time, Forrest is trying to organize a third division under Generals Abraham Buford, Dan W. Adams, Philip D. Roddey and others. But this command will never reach its full strength, as many of the men who were to be included here were sent to Mobile to defend against Canby's advance. Abraham Buford is a lover of horses, especially the Thoroughbreds he breeds in his home state of Kentucky. Portly with sad, sleepy eyes, he is another graduate of West Point and has served well under Old Bedford since early 1864. Dan Adams is the younger brother of Wirt Adams, of Chalmers's division, and commands the District of Central Alabama. He's led a somewhat perilous life. Even before the war, he killed a newspaper editor in a duel for writing a critical article about his father. And while fighting in the heat of the Battle of Shiloh, he lost his right eye. Also, there's Philip Roddey, a self-made man with a hardscrabble past that included various odd jobs ranging from a steamboat crewman to a sheriff. Although lacking in formal schooling, he has developed into a natural military man who recruited his own regiment and participated in many important cavalry raids.[36]

Philip Roddey, incidentally, is also the man who for months has had the tiresome responsibility of watching the Yankee general Wilson gathering and training his troops in North Alabama. While most of Forrest's troops were enjoying their furloughs, Roddey's troops scouted the enemy, sending intelligence reports to Forrest and Taylor along with any other knowledge gained from spies or escaped Confederate prisoners. As Taylor and Forrest continue to compile information about Union plans, they have rightly guessed that the targets would certainly include Selma, although they are not sure whether the attack will come from Canby's forces moving up from Pensacola or from Wilson coming down from the Tennessee River. But with little doubt that one or the other of these forces would move against Selma, Forrest begins moving some troops toward that city shortly after his February meeting with Parkhurst when they discussed the exchange of prisoners.[37]

By the first week of March, Taylor and Forrest have become convinced that Wilson will move into Central Alabama with the aim of destroying the foundries and ordnance operations in Selma and the surrounding areas. So, on March 16, they hold a council of war meeting at Forrest's headquarters in West Point, Mississippi. All the division commanders—Chalmers, Jackson and Buford—are present. Forrest gives instructions as to what must be accomplished to prepare for the upcoming campaign. He makes it clear that rations for at least five days must be made available, that pontoon bridges would have to be built over some of the swollen rivers and that signs would need to be erected along the way instructing the troops what roads to follow to get to the places that must be defended. However, most importantly, the loose network of troops spread out over so vast a territory must be quickly united to defend against the threatened areas.[38]

Suddenly, though, a new development occurs, causing Forrest to momentarily forget about Selma and its environs: one of Canby's columns, twelve thousand infantrymen under Frederick Steele, has left Pensacola, Florida, on March 20, moving north toward Central Alabama. Although the movement is only designed to be a feint toward the region, Forrest reacts to it—just as the Union brass hoped he would—and begins sending his units south to meet the threat. Thus, on March 22, the same day Wilson is moving his columns into northwest Alabama, Forrest is deceived into believing his biggest threat will come from the south. By the time he realizes his mistake, it's March 26, and Wilson has gained a four-day march on him. Immediately, he dispatches riders racing across the countryside to recall the units back toward Selma. Forrest has lost precious time. For the first time, he is in grave danger of breaking his own rule to "get there first with the most men."[39]

Chapter 3

An Inhospitable Land

In beginning the invasion I started my columns on divergent routes for the purpose of confusing the enemy," writes Wilson as he recalls their odyssey across Alabama. This, of course, will prove to be a wise choice for the young general since Forrest's forces are so widely dispersed. And Forrest, not knowing which of these columns might strike first, will be "slow in divining my movement and still be slower in concentrating to resist it."

So, without resistance, three blue columns, each made up of a "well organized" division, move southeastwardly on March 22, traveling on generally parallel routes. Watching them in admiration, Wilson never hesitates to brag about the division and brigade commanders, calling them "natural leaders of the highest quality…capable of overcoming every obstacle they might encounter and of accomplishing every task that might fall to their lot." The First Division, occupying the right and composed of just over four thousand men, is led by Edward M. McCook. Although he's "unusually handsome, strong, and vigorous," he has had little formal training in military art. But his wartime experience is excellent, having served in the Atlanta Campaign, where he "made his name a horror" for Southerners there. His division, like the others, is composed of two brigades. "Tall, handsome, dark-eyed" John T. Croxton has charge of the First Brigade. A Yale-educated Kentuckian, Croxton has, according to Wilson, "distinguished himself for coolness and courage in action." In this next campaign, as will be seen, he will play a major role. McCook's other brigade is commanded by Oscar H.

LaGrange, a powerfully built man from New York who, Wilson says, is "one of the best all-around soldiers I ever met."[40]

The largest division in Wilson's force belongs to Eli Long. With more than five thousand men, it occupies the center position. Long, a Kentuckian by birth, is a "serious, deliberate and methodical" sort of man. Although those serving with him usually find him to be quiet and modest, in battle he can become as "dreadful as the storm." He's fortunate, or so Wilson believes, to have as one of his brigade commanders Robert H.G. Minty, an Irishman whose father was a British officer and who, like his father, has served the Crown in many stations around the world. The blond-haired Minty is the beau ideal of a cavalryman—smart, well educated, dashing and flamboyant. Wilson sees him as "natty and debonair…a dandy cavalryman." The other brigade in Long's division is not actually cavalry but rather mounted infantry. Originally known as "Wilder's Lightning Brigade," it's one of the most famed units in Civil War history and is now commanded by Abram Miller. "A doctor by profession but a soldier by instinct and preference," says Wilson, who adds a glowing tribute to the Indiana colonel: "Steady as a clock and as intrepid as the best grenadier of them all."[41]

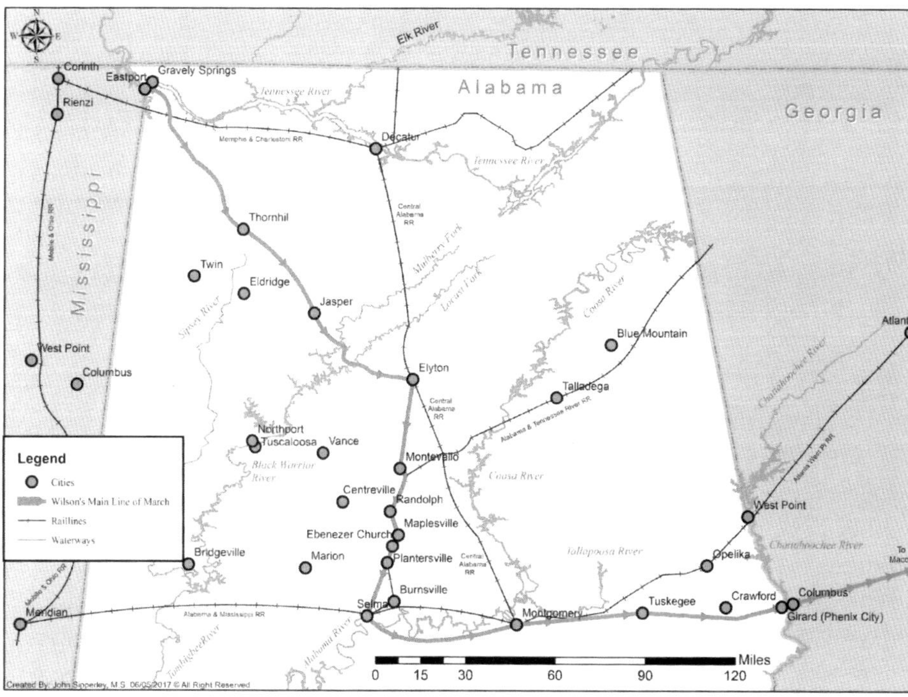

Map of Wilson's Raid. *Produced by John Sipperly.*

Emory Upton leads the column positioned on the left. A New Yorker, he has commanded infantry, artillery and cavalry during the war and "has seldom, if ever, had his record equaled." After Upton recovered from a wound suffered in Virginia, Wilson requested that he be transferred to his command, knowing him to be "one of the most accomplished and aggressive soldiers of his time." Edward F. Winslow leads Upton's First Brigade. Only twenty-eight years old and from a very distinguished family in Maine, Winslow is a seasoned veteran of many battlefields nevertheless. The remaining brigade falls under the leadership of Andrew Alexander, another Kentuckian who had served as Wilson's chief of staff before being recommended for the position of brigadier.[42]

In addition to these three mounted divisions, there are, of course, other elements of Wilson's caravan. Each division is accompanied by an artillery battery of four guns, all of which are manned by experienced cannoneers such as the acclaimed Chicago Board of Trade Battery, assisting Long's division. As in any wartime invasion, there is also a number of support personnel, including surgeons, corpsmen, cooks, clerical staff and even a few superfluous persons such as the musicians in the regimental bands. In the rear of the columns are 1,500 dismounted men, trudging along with the supply train of 250 wagons and a pontoon train of boats hauled by fifty-six teams of mules. Because the wagons are "a great impediment to cavalry," Wilson has ordered them to be sent back one by one as soon as they're emptied of their supplies and rations. As the column makes its way south, Wilson hopes that enough horses will be captured along the way to mount the 1,500 men who are on foot, thus enabling his force to move more rapidly. And for Wilson, like his adversary, Forrest, celerity of movement is essential in military operations. "That force which moves most rapidly," insists Wilson, "can place itself in the best position for effective service."[43]

As soon as their journey begins, it's apparent to everyone that the gnarly country of North Alabama is sterile and destitute in every direction. Some might even call it Mother Nature's poorhouse. Wilson describes it as a "hilly, gravelly, and barren region, covered with dense forests of pine and oak, broken here and there by the small clearings of poor white folks." In addition to being "sandy and barren," the entire land has already been ravaged and devastated by roaming armies. There is hardly anything for the Union cavalrymen or their animals to eat except the rations in their haversacks and whatever is carried on the wagons. "Hood's army had pretty well cleaned the region of grain," notices one disappointed Iowa cavalryman in Upton's division. But even before the war, in the best of times, the land was generally inhospitable for farming or little else.[44]

The population here, like the knobby landscape, is impoverished and depleted. "The people wear homespun and are generally quite ignorant," remarks Charles Wooster, a young private in a Michigan unit. Surprisingly, "The citizens had never seen Yankees before and were badly scared," according to E.N. Gilpin, a clerk for General Upton. Wooster agrees, claiming, "That they often took our men for Rebels, not acting as though they had ever heard of such a thing as a U.S. uniform." Beyond that, few of the people Wilson's troops encounter in this part of the country have much interest in the war, even less in the ideology behind it. Most are ignorant, surly and only concerned with their day-to-day survival in a land that holds little promise for body and soul. For them, relevance is consumed by crop failure, debt, poverty and unexplainable deaths in their families. The intrusion of a large body of troops, such as this huge cavalry procession, doesn't happen every day on the farm and, in some cases, causes great consternation. One such incident occurs when Wooster's Michigan unit stops at one of the crude farmhouses to feed their horses. During the stop, a regimental band accompanying the troops begins playing a favorite martial tune. Immediately, "an old man came running up from the fields in a great fright," remembers Wooster, "probably thinking that some horrid thing from the infernal regions had appeared on earth. As soon as he became a little cool, in answer to inquiries, he stated that he had never heard a band before and didn't know what it was."[45]

During the first five days of the march, Wilson's columns cover about one hundred miles, a respectable distance for such a large body of cavalry considering the rough terrain and poor roads. This first leg of their journey has not been, as Wilson curtly declares, "without anxiety." Numerous difficulties have continually impeded their progress. Although the constant rains have stopped, there are bridgeless creeks and streams, swollen out of their banks, that must be forded. Roads in the low areas have become quagmires, horses and mules flounder in the mire and men struggle, pushing and pulling wagons and caissons through the morass. Delays are constant since the men must stop and corduroy the roads that have become impassable. Still, there is at least some good fortune in these first days of the expedition. The weather has finally turned pleasant, and with it the first signs of spring appear as trees and vegetation begin rioting in bloom. What's more, they have yet to meet any real enemy resistance. Forrest, thankfully, has thus far not appeared. Nonetheless, Wilson will remain vigilant. "Forrest," he admits, is "an aggressive and swiftly marching enemy, and no one could tell when we might find him in the front."[46]

On March 27, the blue skies give way to more rain. Near noon, long lines of Yankee horsemen covered in ponchos trot into the town of Jasper, the county seat of Walker County. Here, Upton's and McCook's divisions converge with Eli Long's center column. And it's here in Jasper where Wilson first learns that Forrest is on the move, having left Mississippi and now riding hard with his escort to intercept the invaders. Taylor and Forrest, finally realizing their mistake—that the threat to Central Alabama will not be from Canby but from Wilson's cavalry—have recalled and redirected the Rebel cavalry, sending Buford's troops to Montevallo and the divisions of Chalmers and Jackson to Tuscaloosa and Selma. But Wilson knows that all these movements will take time since the Rebels are "badly scattered." And now, since the rains have returned, streams and rivers will swell and roads will be ruined, further hampering the shifting of their cavalry. Thus, he's convinced he can reach his objectives before they can countermarch to impede his progress. "The race was now on for Selma," says the young general. To win that race, he knows they must travel faster than before and says so: "We should quicken our own speed so as to cross the Cahaba and reach the district about Montevallo before the enemy could interpose to delay us." However, before they cross the Cahaba River, or even reach the next town, the village of Elyton, they must cross two major forks of the Black Warrior River, which is a treacherous natural barrier.[47]

Later that day, the leading elements of the Union cavalry reach the first of the river forks of the Black Warrior, known as Mulberry Fork. It's a wide and rapid stream, flowing through a steep-sided gorge with a rocky bottom, making it difficult for the horses to keep their footing. It's understandable, then, that the Union commander, Upton, is hesitant about crossing without a pontoon bridge. Unwilling to spend the time waiting for the train of boats to catch up with the column, he decides to go ahead and ford these waters. Such a perilous undertaking naturally attracts a number of local civilians, who gather on the banks "to watch the fun." There is even a small band playing as they plunge into the river, and every time a dripping soldier and his horse stagger up the opposite bank, the band blares and the onlookers cheer. Clerk Gilpin, in Upton's division, sees that most of the men succeed in crossing safely, but he later remarks, "Many had fallen into the river, some swimming, others clinging to the rocks, and some plunging far down where the channel ran between precipitous banks at the mercy of the foaming waters." At times, when the soldiers are swept from their horses, many are fortunate enough to grab the tail of the next animal and convey themselves across. All in all, crossing the forks of the Black Warrior is a remarkable venture. After the last of the great procession clears Locust Fork, the second and less daunting fork of the Black Warrior, Wilson is relieved that his losses are but few, reporting that "[s]everal troopers were swept away and one was drowned before assistance could reach him." One grateful rider, after barely making it to safety, was reluctant to attempt it in the first place and sums up his harrowing experience with the understatement: "Quite an interesting proceeding to one not accustomed to such things."[48]

With the natural barriers behind them, Wilson's troops trot into the town of Elyton on March 30, a cloudy and cold day. "A very pretty village of 3,000 to 4,000 inhabitants," according to Union surgeon Francis Salter. General Wilson, however, doesn't share that assessment, calling it "[p]overty-stricken and uninviting…a poor insignificant Southern village, surrounded by old field farms, most of which could be bought at five dollars per acre." But notwithstanding their opinions of the town, neither man could imagine that it would one day become the most important iron and steel center in the American South: Birmingham, Alabama.[49]

By the time Wilson reaches Elyton, Forrest and Taylor are well aware that the Federal horsemen are closing in on their true objectives of Tuscaloosa, Selma and Montgomery. All of Forrest's cavalry have been redirected to concentrate as many men as possible to join him and defend these targets, especially Selma, against the Yankee threat. In fact, Red Jackson's division is already moving past the town of Tuscaloosa and heading for Centerville. Their journey from Mississippi has been difficult, moving day and night "over muddy roads, miry swamps and rugged hills." Jackson's men are all Tennessee veterans, and although they're "a long way from home" and not sure of their exact destination, they are "ready for a last desperate struggle in a strange land." Along the way, they're reminded that Forrest, who is riding with his escort a day ahead of them, is becoming "greatly exasperated" with an increasing number of desertions. Even the Yankee cavalry hear rumors of Forrest's anger over desertions, prompting Wilson to write, "His blood was up."[50]

Crossing the bridge at Sipsey River, Jackson's column comes upon some guards left behind by Forrest with strict orders to arrest any soldier coming through the country without proper orders or authority. From the guards, they learn that two soldiers had been arrested the day before by Forrest's troops when his escort had passed through. The men were Kentuckians and apparently not part of Forrest's command. After admitting they had been in the service but were quitting the army and going home, Forrest ordered them to be court-martialed. One of the men then claimed to be too old for service, while the other argued that he was too young for military duty. Nevertheless, they were tried, condemned and executed.[51]

The next day, Private John Hubbard, riding with Jackson's provost guard at the rear of the column, passes through what he describes as a "weird looking place," in an area where the woods were dark from the heavy foliage, shutting out the sunlight. There, Hubbard sees the two men and relates the scene: "Dead men lying one on each side of the road with their heads against trees. Their hats had been placed over their faces, but labels written in large letters told the story: Shot for Desertion." Hubbard calls the execution "extremely unfortunate" since the men's stories about their ages "turned out to be true in every particular."[52]

Although most of the Rebel cavalrymen would agree that these executions were, in fact, "extremely unfortunate," they realize that Forrest is using such extreme measures as a desertion deterrent. Now, especially, he needs every man in his command. But Frank Montgomery, a Mississippian in Chalmers's division, remains skeptical about the effectiveness of the executions. He tells of witnessing another "poor fellow shot for desertion a short time ago" and then adds the caveat, "I fear it has failed to check the evil." And as important as it is for Forrest to keep every man in the ranks, Montgomery, thinking back on it, despondently confesses, "But if we could have had them all, we could not have defeated the overwhelming force our enemy had; no, not if we could have had every man in the south would we be able now to cope with this force."[53]

This same "overwhelming force" is now at Elyton, where Wilson is preparing to carry out the mission he has been sent to accomplish: the total destruction of all military, private or public facilities lying in his path that could possibly contribute to the Confederate cause. Having left his wagons in the wild and rugged land between the two forks of the Black Warrior River and guarded by his dismounted troops, Wilson is now free to move fast and hit hard. Even before reaching Elyton, his raiders have put the torch to their first target, Lamson's Flour Mills. And in and around Elyton, five blast furnaces are destroyed. These will be the first in a long list of demolished ordnance and manufacturing centers, iron blast furnaces, textile mills, rolling mills, steamboats, railroads, shot and shell foundries, niter works and powder mills in their rampage through Alabama. Even though Wilson forbids his troops to destroy private property with no military value, it happens, and frequently. A large military force such as Wilson's, traveling through enemy territory, is often impossible to control. This is especially true in areas where enemy troops offer resistance. In such cases as Wilson's Raid or Sherman's March to the Sea, communities are held responsible for any Rebel attacks in the area of their town. Thus, it becomes a sort of malicious custom among the Federal soldiers to destroy private property as a penalty or retribution against the people.[54]

Wilson's last act before leaving Elyton is to dispatch a full brigade of cavalry toward Tuscaloosa, one of Grant's mandated targets. What's more, Wilson believes the movement of a brigade in that direction might serve to bewilder Forrest and his command in their pursuit of his raiders. He turns to Edward McCook for this mission, giving him the following orders: "Detach one brigade of your division, with orders to proceed rapidly by the most direct route to Tuscaloosa to destroy the bridge, factories, mills, university (military school) and whatever else may be of benefit to the Rebel cause. As soon as this work is accomplished, instruct the commanding officer to join the corps by the Centerville Road."[55]

It's hardly surprising that McCook picks the Kentuckian John Croxton and his brigade for such a hazardous mission. Wilson can only agree with McCook's choice, describing Croxton as "an officer of rare discretion, coolness and courage, always ready for any duty that might be assigned him." This assignment will prove to be especially dangerous since neither Wilson nor Croxton are aware that Jackson's division of Rebel cavalry is at this time near Tuscaloosa. Croxton's brigade is made up of 1,500 veterans from Iowa, Michigan and Kentucky, all armed with Spencer carbines and each carrying 120 rounds of ammunition. But Jackson's division, veterans too, outnumbers the Yankee brigade, having about 2,600 horsemen. Croxton will need an enormous amount of luck to succeed in this endeavor.

For Harry Wilson, the mission will be the source of much anxiety before it's over. The young general watches Croxton and his brigade disappear from sight at four o'clock on the afternoon of March 30. As they ride away, he cannot know that he will not see them again until May 1, when they will

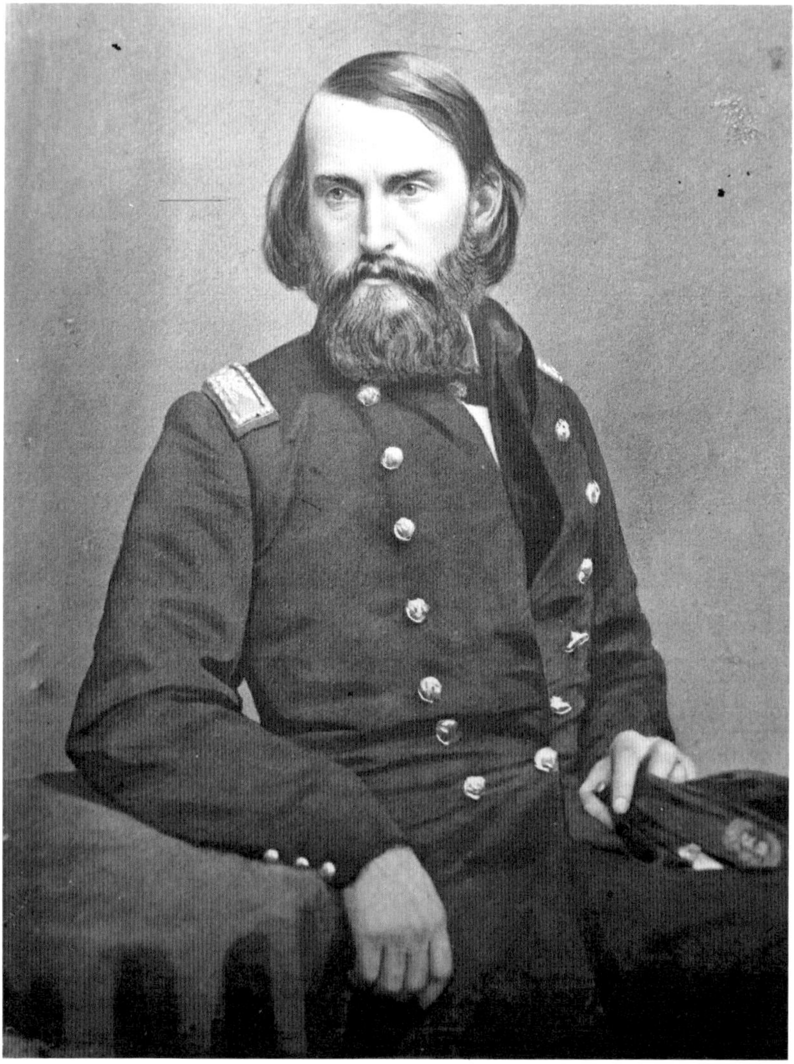

Union general John Croxton commanded the "Lost Brigade" during Wilson's campaign. *Courtesy Library of Congress.*

rejoin the main column at Macon, Georgia. Nor can Croxton know that he will not communicate with Wilson's main force or be heard from for a month. During this time, they will wander 653 miles, meandering through enemy territory, often without supplies, and subsisting in a destitute country. But despite their arduous escapade, the "Lost Brigade," as it will come to be called, will somehow succeed in accomplishing its mission.[56]

Chapter 4

The Lost Brigade

Without the impediment of dragging artillery and a long wagon train behind them, Croxton's column leaves Elyton and moves swiftly toward the town of Tuscaloosa, which is about seventy miles to the southwest. Even though the roads are "wretched," according to Croxton, the brigade covers eight miles in the afternoon and evening of March 30 before going into camp. Traveling light, it's only burdened with one baggage wagon, three ambulance wagons and a small number of pack mules. Thus, Croxton is expecting to make good time in his journey, and based on what he believes to be a reliable source, he won't be hampered by enemy resistance along the way. Before leaving Elyton, a judge and Union loyalist named Mudd, who had just visited Tuscaloosa, told him there was not a Confederate force in the area and that the town was only defended by militia and university cadets.[57]

Breaking camp early the next morning, March 31, the brigade trots ahead. Along the way, near the present-day town of Bessemer, Croxton dispatches three companies of horsemen to destroy the nearby Saunder's Iron Works, which for the past two years had been manufacturing "ordnance and all the munitions of war, as well as pots, pans, and skillets, all for the Confederacy." It's the first target to be destroyed, but only one of several other factories, mills and stores that are burned this same day. Aside from accomplishing this destruction, the day begins rather uneventfully. However, unknown to Croxton, he will soon discover that he's about to be surrounded by Rebels. His brigade is blindly pushing into the path of Red Jackson's Rebel division.[58]

At about five o'clock in the afternoon, the raiders are approaching the village of Trion, which is only twenty miles from Tuscaloosa. Watching from a wooded hilltop, Croxton's advance scouts spot the rear of Jackson's division, dragging artillery and moving south toward Centerville to protect the river crossings there. This presents a dilemma for Croxton, something he had not contemplated. Pondering what he should do next, he first decides to follow the Rebel column during the night, seeking a chance to attack it from the rear. But shortly thereafter, Croxton receives more reports from his scouts, telling him that he's outnumbered. Prudently, he changes his mind again, resolving to obey Wilson's orders and go on to Tuscaloosa.[59]

Croxton then turns the column around and goes into camp for the night. But by this time, Red Jackson is aware of the presence of a Yankee column behind him. At 8:45 p.m., he sends word to Forrest, advising him of the situation: "I am closing around them with the view of attacking at daylight in the morning." At the same time, Jackson sends a courier to Tuscaloosa with a warning to be on guard for the Yankee column. Finally, he dispatches part of his force to get between Croxton and Tuscaloosa, just in case something goes wrong.[60]

Croxton can now think only of extricating himself from what might well become a disaster. Shrewdly, he breaks camp before daylight, reverses his direction away from Tuscaloosa and slips down the Mud Creek Road toward the Black Warrior River. However, before all of his 1,500 men can break camp and complete the withdrawal, Jackson strikes with a fury. The Confederate cavalrymen romp over the camp, killing and capturing a number of the bluecoats, along with their horses and the ambulances. In full flight, with Jackson's horsemen right behind them, Croxton and his brigade finally manage to escape. After chasing the blue column for several miles, Jackson decides to break off his pursuit and move again toward Centerville. After he's satisfied that the bluecoats are "scattered in the mountains," the ever-chivalrous Red Jackson, who has always been popular with the citizens of Tuscaloosa, takes the time to send a dispatch to the officer commanding the militia there. "Assure the fair ladies of Tuscaloosa," he crows, "that the tread of the vandal hordes shall not pollute the streets of their beautiful city."[61]

By sundown on April 1, the "Lost Brigade," exhausted from a hard forty-mile flight, has arrived at Johnson's Ferry on the banks of the Black Warrior River. It's been a grueling jaunt, but it is now reunited and a safe distance away from the Rebel cavalry. But the retreat has carried the men forty miles away from their objective of Tuscaloosa. Croxton knows he must come up with a new strategy for accomplishing his mission. However, he doesn't know the whereabouts of Jackson's cavalry, which, in fact, is now moving away from him to protect river crossing at Centerville before joining Forrest at Plantersville to defeat Wilson's main column. Croxton also does not know that he has already unwittingly helped Wilson by delaying Jackson's march to Centerville. That delay allows Wilson time to send Edward McCook racing to Centerville to seize and destroy the Cahaba River Bridge, thus keeping Jackson from uniting with Forrest.[62]

Facing these new circumstances, the resourceful Croxton decides to alter his original plan. He will cross the river here at Johnson's Ferry and follow the road that runs southwestwardly along the river to the town of Northport, lying across the river from Tuscaloosa. Here, a vital bridge spans the river, and Croxton intends to capture it from the sentinels under the cover of darkness and then rush into the town of Tuscaloosa from the north in a surprise attack.[63]

Although his men are bone-tired from their strenuous ride, the young brigadier decides to waste no time and continues moving. Without rest, his weary men begin crossing the Black Warrior this same Saturday night. Having only one flatboat, numerous trips are necessary to ferry the men and wagons across the river. The horses, however, are forced to swim across, and that proves difficult since the river is thirty feet higher than its normal stage. In spite of the fact that Croxton only reports losing "two or three" horses in the crossing, civilians in Tuscaloosa later claim that two bodies of drowned men and several horses washed up in a bend a few miles below the city. All night long and through the next day of April 2, the crossing continues. Finally, by sunset, the entire command is across the river, where it goes into camp for a well-deserved breather before having to make another forced march of forty miles to Tuscaloosa.[64]

At first light, Monday morning, they mount up and follow the river road toward Northport. Along the way, any civilians found traveling on the road have their journeys interrupted by arrest just to make sure the raiders' presence will not be disclosed to the Confederate authorities. Earlier, Croxton had dispatched a number of spies, dressed in Confederate uniforms, to infiltrate the town and report the troop strength and artillery available to defend the place. Dr. William S. Wyman remembers seeing "several men sitting in the front part of the Presbyterian Church; the parties were strangers and wore the Confederate gray, and naturally they passed for some of our soldiers." A few days later, a lady in the choir tells of being accosted by a Union soldier who admitted to her that he was one of the men in the front row of the church on Sunday.[65]

By nine o'clock on the moonlit night of April 3, Croxton and his men have reached the outskirts of Northport. Halting in a cedar grove, where the column stretches back a mile and a half down the road, Croxton picks 150 men from the Second Michigan to dismount and quietly follow him toward the river. Among the Michigan troopers is twenty-two-year-old Charles Wooster, who, along with another man, volunteer to capture the guard at the bridge. Describing the stealthy mission, Wooster gives his account: "[We] divest ourselves of all superfluous equipment which might impede our movements, leave our guns and each with a revolver in his hand and a Negro to guide us, start for the bridge, followed by good support within hearing distance." But as they approach the bridge, Croxton, leading the support, cocks his ear to the sounds of Confederate troops tearing the planking off the bridge: "I could distinctly hear the rebels removing the flooring in the bridge." Thinking the Rebels had somehow learned they were approaching, he knows he must act quickly to keep them from destroying it and orders his soldiers to rush the bridge. Led by Lieutenant Colonel Thomas Johnston, the Michigan men, according to Croxton's official report, "[r]ushed into the bridge, halted for nothing until they had killed and captured the whole of the guard and had possession of the bridge." Afterward, Private Wooster estimates that "there were 14 rebels" and then adds, "There was some pretty sharp firing, but we were so fortunate as to lose only two killed and some few wounded."[66]

With the bridge secure, the door to Tuscaloosa is wide open. Croxton immediately sends fifty men running "double quick" to a stable in the center of town, where they seize two pieces of artillery stored there for the use of the cadets and militia in case of an invasion. In all probability, Croxton learned of these guns and their location from one of his spies. While the raiders are busy confiscating the guns, wagons, horses and other supplies from the stable, another group of dismounted bluecoats is repairing the twenty feet of planking ripped from the bridge. Sometime around midnight, the entire command crosses the repaired overpass to the Tuscaloosa side of the river, but not before burning the Olmstead Hat Factory, which was guilty of producing gray wool hats for the Confederacy.[67]

In addition to the hat factory, Tuscaloosa is also the site of other factories, a foundry, two niter works, warehouses and a number of government stores that are supplying rations for the Confederacy. However, the town's most significant target, at least in the eyes of the Union generals, is the University of Alabama. Since the beginning of the war, Federal authorities have considered that university to be a "military school" because it has maintained a corps of cadets who, upon graduation, have gone into the service of the Confederacy as officers. However, by now, late in the war, most of the upperclassmen have already left the school before graduating and enlisted in the army. Only three companies of young cadets remain, and they are mere boys—"katydids," the veteran soldiers call them, in a joking reference to their insect-like resemblance when attired in their dress uniforms.[68]

The first to notice the Yankee marauders darting through the streets of the city is Pat Kehoe, supervisor of Bryce Hospital. His uppermost concern is to get word to the cadet corps at the university, and he hurries off in that direction. After alerting Dr. Landon Garland, president of the university, and Colonel James Murfee, commandant of the cadets, Kehoe rushes on to the hospital and sounds the alarm. Soon after, the sound of a drummer beating the "long roll" resonates across campus, rushing three hundred cadets into formation. Led by Garland and Murfee, the young soldiers, along with several professors, faculty members and a few local militiamen, march into town. Along the way, they learn that their artillery has already been seized. Moving on, determined to meet the enemy with only their rifles, they meet the first of the enemy regiments, which happens to be the Sixth Kentucky Cavalry.

In the darkness, the cadets are unaware of the size of the force in their path. Shots are fired from both sides, and the Southern boys are ordered to lie flat down on the ground. Other than one cadet being wounded in the foot, the firing has little effect. But Dr. Garland is now convinced that he is facing a much larger force than his students can cope with and prudently orders everyone back to campus. Once there, they immediately blow up one of the magazines storing their spare ammunition. Fortunately, the Union troops have not pursued the cadets, and that allows them enough time to gather supplies, pack their knapsacks and begin marching out of Tuscaloosa en route to Marion, Alabama, where they will soon be disbanded. Sadly, although they have no reason to suspect it as they depart, Dr. Garland and his cadets will never see the old buildings of their university again.[69]

Although this night turns into one filled with anxious fear, destruction and even death for the people of Tuscaloosa, for some, at least, it doesn't begin that way. On Fourth Street, near the river, dozens of horse-drawn carriages and buggies are parked in one of the town's most affluent neighborhoods. Inside the home of Dr. Sewell Leach an elegant wedding is taking place, and the guests are all assembled to witness the marriage of the doctor's daughter, Emily, to a handsome young Confederate officer, Captain James Carpenter.[70]

Elite, high-browed folks from Tuscaloosa's best families crowd through the parlors and hallways. The groom and his attendants, all soldiers, are wearing their best uniforms and escorting bridesmaids donned in their finest dresses. The evening is special, filled with memories of forgotten romances, a throwback to more genteel days before the war had devastated their lives. Because of these harsh times, the ceremony, dinner and drinks are not nearly as elegant as they once were. Nevertheless, everyone is carefree, in good spirits and enjoying the moment.

That moment comes to an abrupt end shortly after nine o'clock, when the sounds of gunshots begin ringing out in the direction of the Northport Bridge. Right away, the wedding party knows that the terror of war has finally come to their town. The firing draws closer, mounting to a crescendo until bullets are striking the house. Outside in the street, the night is bursting into riotous bedlam. Black coachmen are fleeing for their lives, while carriage horses, hit by stray shots, are dropping dead in their harnesses. Knowing it's a matter of minutes before the enemy is swarming inside the house and the looting begins, the male guests hastily remove their valuables for the ladies to hide in their slippers and the garments beneath their bustles.[71]

After rushing through the front door, the blue raiders immediately arrest all the men, who willingly surrender rather than make a stand in what would clearly be a senseless struggle. Dr. Leach, an elderly man and evidently not in good health, is spared from being made a prisoner and continues to try and calm his frantic guests. At the first sight of the intruders barging into the house, the bride and her maids flee upstairs. There they remain as soldiers begin ransacking the home and guards herd the men out, taking them across the river to the Yankee camp in Northport. Among the prisoners is the groom, Captain Carpenter, who after being prodded into the enemy camp insists on speaking with General Croxton. The general then listens to the woeful tale of a ruined wedding, the bride left behind and the plea of Carpenter to be paroled and go back to his new wife. Both men are from Kentucky and, by chance, even know of each other. And that, perhaps, has something to do with Croxton being persuaded to allow the young officer to return to his bride, Emily, on the condition that he will not try to escape and agree to the terms of a parole.[72]

The next morning, Tuscaloosa's mayor, Obediah Berry, accompanied by Father William McDonough, a local Catholic priest, make their way through the shattered sites of the town, down to the river crossing, and plant a white flag in the ground to proclaim that the city is now surrendered. Customarily, a white flag is treated as a plea for leniency and protection from the victors against further violence and destruction. Such merciful treatment, though, will not be forthcoming. Croxton has his instructions, and they are explicit orders to destroy.[73]

By nine o'clock this same morning, Croxton's horsemen are storming over the grounds of the university. The cadets, of course, have already evacuated along with most of the professors, who have accompanied them to Marion. Riding from building to building, the raiders methodically put the torch to each one until little remains but the president's mansion, the Gorgas home and the observatory, which are somehow saved through the brave efforts of the women on campus. Approaching the fine old library, the raiders are met by Andrew Delorffe, professor of modern languages, who begins pleading with the Federal officer in charge to spare the Rotunda housing the magnificent collection of books. The officer, who is apparently "a man of culture and of literary taste," seems to sympathize and even agree with Delorffe's appeal. He summons a courier and sends him to Croxton with a note saying that it would be pathetic to destroy such an academic landmark. Soon, the courier returns bearing Croxton's answer: his orders are "imperative" and he has "no discretion in the matter." Disappointed, the officer calls it "a pity" and then reluctantly orders the building burned. Strange as it may seem, before the torch is applied the officer pulls a book from the shelves as a memento of the library. It happens to be a copy of the Koran.[74]

Now, most of the university's buildings are engulfed in flames—Washington, Jefferson, Franklin and Madison Halls and finally the Rotunda. Billows of smoke cover the campus, rising so high in the windless sky that they can be seen by the cadets, who are by this time miles away. The young soldiers then hear one final, deafening explosion, signaling that the main powder magazine has been blown up. Burning debris is hurled through the air, setting fire to private homes nearby. The official Federal records do not report the burning of any nonmilitary targets. And yet, Belle Harrison, only a young girl at the time, remembers being in one of the homes that caught fire. Years later, another young witness, Thomas Clinton, recalls, "I watched the buildings as they gave way to the angry flames, and it made an impression on my youthful mind that was lasting in its effects." "Beyond all question," declares Clinton, "it was the greatest fire I ever witnessed, and probably greater than I will ever see again."[75]

Leaving the university in an inferno behind them, Croxton's raiders spend the rest of the afternoon and the next day completing their mission of destruction. First and closest to the college is the niter works, manufacturing saltpeter, or potassium nitrate, a chemical compound in gunpowder. Due to a spell of very dry weather, it burns rapidly, as do all the sites to be destroyed. Sweeping on through the countryside, one target after another is put to the torch: the Black Warrior Cotton Factory along with two cotton warehouses; a corn warehouse; the Foster Tannery; the Roupes Valley Iron Works; and the Leach and Avery Foundry, manufacturing munitions and soldiers' hats and owned by none other than the hapless Dr. Sewell Leach, who has just had his house ransacked during the wedding of his daughter.[76]

By April 5, Croxton has accomplished his mission, resupplied his troops with all the confiscated rations they can carry and—for whatever it's worth—taken $1 million in currency from the office of the Confederate States Depository. He is ready to leave Tuscaloosa. But where should he go? For the young brigadier, there is much that troubles him. He's received no word from his commander, Wilson, since leaving Elyton. He has no idea of Wilson's progress in taking Selma. And although Wilson's instructions were for him to cross the Cahaba River at Centerville and rejoin the corps at Selma, he has no idea of the whereabouts of Red Jackson's Rebels. They may be at Centerville, or they may be preparing to pounce on him here in Tuscaloosa. After all, many rumors have been circulating among the townspeople that Jackson is on his way. The *Tuscaloosa Observer* is said to have reported, "Some young men coming in to town with their horses in a run…waving their hats and yelling in a loud voice, 'Hurrah for Jackson! Jackson is coming.'" As a last straw, an elderly lady pays a visit to Croxton's headquarters, warning him in an authoritative, almost bossy manner that Jackson is only a few miles away from town and coming this way.[77]

One cannot be sure how much these alarming rumors and stories influence Croxton's decision to hurry his departure, but the young Kentuckian is clearly anxious to move his brigade out of Tuscaloosa. "I determined to recross the Black Warrior," he writes in his report, "and if possible to destroy the railroad between Demopolis and Meridian." In other words, the only direction open to him, in keeping with his orders, is southwest. This, of course, will mean moving farther away from Wilson and the main corps, traveling into unfamiliar territory and living off the land. The reality is that he and his 1,500 men have, indeed, become a lost brigade.[78]

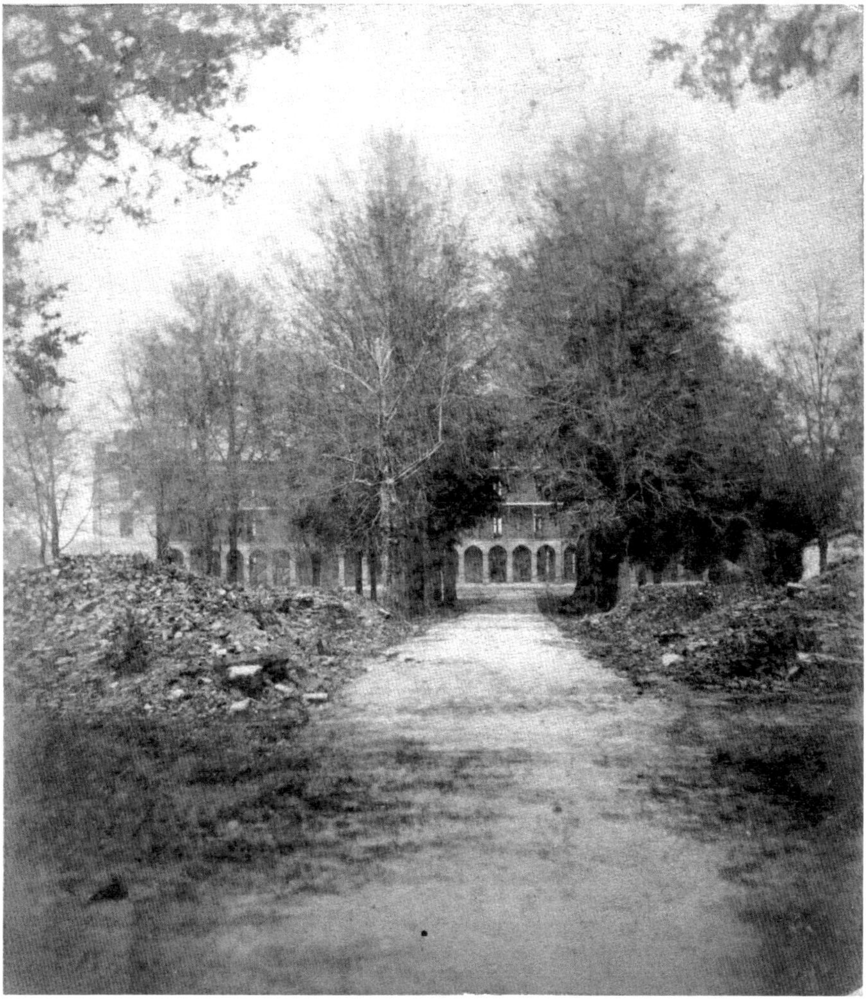

Ruins of the University of Alabama in the aftermath of Croxton's Raid. *Courtesy Alabama Department of Archives and History, Montgomery Alabama.*

To the delight and relief of the citizens, Croxton leads his brigade out of Tuscaloosa on April 5. Leaving by the same route they entered, the column crosses the bridge over Black Warrior River to Northport. Then, in one final incendiary act, Croxton orders the bridge burned behind them. Watching their departure, some of the townspeople rejoice in a celebration, gathering around the flagpole on the drill ground and "singing Dixie and the Bonny Blue Flag." Most, however, find little reason to rejoice. In less than two days, there has been at least $1 million of damage done to their property.

Homes have burned, along with the state's fine university. Horses, mules and other livestock are confiscated, and untold quantities of personal property, including gold, is stolen during the plunder of the town. Moreover, there has been human suffering. Although there is no accurate count, men have died and been wounded and more than seventy taken prisoner. In the end, the total loss of lives and property suffered by the people of Tuscaloosa costs Croxton twenty-three men, either killed or wounded.[79]

Looking back on all the mayhem, carnage and devastation the city has just been through a few days later, Captain Aaron Hardcastle sits down and writes his report to the Confederate authorities. In it, he gives his account of the surprise attack, the destruction and the losses. Hardcastle, after all, is the officer in charge of the town's defenses and, ultimately, the man the government holds responsible for protecting the city from the Yankee hordes. But except for the cadets, who were actually not under his authority, all he had for military resistance was the home guard or local militia, which amounted to nothing more than a few old men and pimple-faced boys, unfit for duty in the regular army. What's more, the hope of a rescue by Red Jackson's troops never materialized. Thus, when he ends his report, he does so with a sorrowful explanation: "I did the best I could with the means I had."[80]

Chapter 5

THE ROAD TO SELMA

As Croxton's "Lost Brigade" is accomplishing its mission of destruction in Tuscaloosa, Wilson's main body of troops is continuing to move south, pressing toward the remainder of the objectives. In the van of the long column of horsemen is Emory Upton's division, followed by Long's and McCook's divisions. Once across the Cahaba River, between Elyton and Montevallo, the raiders begin to encounter the manufacturing facilities within the iron-rich region of Alabama, an important source of raw materials for the Confederate war arsenal in Selma.

Before the war, little attention had been paid to the industrial potential of the iron ore and coal known to be here. The antebellum South seemed only interested in immediate profits of the land derived from slaves and cotton. However, there were a few visionaries in the prewar South. Men such as J.D.B. DeBow, the South's most celebrated editor, saw the economic possibilities of the state's natural resources and said so. "Like young Hercules in his cradle," crowed *De Bow's Review* in 1855. But the progress was slow. By the outset of the war, Alabama could claim only four furnaces and two rolling mills. The necessities of war, however, changed everything. During the war years, thirteen new furnaces were constructed in the state, bringing the total to seventeen. And by 1865, Alabama is producing more iron for the Confederate war effort than all the seceding states combined. Knowing this, the Federal government believes it to be critical for Wilson to eliminate as many of these facilities as possible.[81]

One by one, the raiders burn or blow up the ironworks, furnaces, mills and collieries in this area. Upton's division, being in the lead, naturally does most of the damage. Even though Philip Roddey tries to watch over the important industrial facilities by spreading his troops around the countryside, they are too few to offer any real protection. As a result, all of them are soon put out of operation, including the Red Mountain Iron Works, the Cahaba Valley Rolling Mills, the Columbiana (Shelby) Iron Works and the Bibb (Brierfield) Naval Furnace. By far, though, the largest and most important iron producer in the Deep South is the Shelby Iron Company. Its destruction is a devastating blow to the Confederacy. Not only do hundreds of workers lose their jobs, but the South is also deprived of the high-quality iron necessary for the factories at Selma to produce its war materiel. Additionally, the Shelby Company has been the only supplier of spike iron, desperately needed for repairing railroads wrecked by Union troops, especially those in Georgia and the Carolinas that happened to lay in Sherman's path. So complete is the damage at the Shelby facilities that A.T. Jones, president of the company, writes an associate afterward, "The Yankees played the devil with things here. Very little of our machinery is worth anything."[82]

Leaving the smoldering ruins behind them on the last day of March, Upton's horsemen finally begin encountering their first real resistance just a few miles south of Montevallo. Here on the Selma Road, where the Rebel cavalry has been driven back to Six Mile Creek, Philip Roddey cobbles together a defense made up of his five Alabama regiments, a fragment of the Kentucky brigade of Colonel Edward Crossland and a handful of infantry militia brought up from Selma by Dan Adams, a one-eyed general nominally in charge of the District of Central Alabama. It's a meager lot and clearly no match for the Yankee raiders, but Roddey nevertheless is doing all he can to buy enough time for Forrest to arrive.[83]

Early in the afternoon, at about 1:00 p.m., Harry Wilson arrives at the front, and Upton apprises him of the situation. Wilson, believing that Forrest is here in person and leading the Rebel defenders, wryly remarks, "Face to face at last." Forrest, however, is not here. Not yet. He is still riding hard from Centerville with his escort of seventy-five men and a few hundred horsemen from Frank Armstrong's brigade. Determined not to let Forrest "strike the first blow," Wilson orders Upton "to sail in." And so he does, with troops from Iowa and Missouri, along with a battery of artillery, assaulting and driving the Rebel horsemen mile after mile, from one position to the next, down the road toward the town of Randolph. Forrest and his men reach the road at a point where the Confederates have already retreated from but where the Union cavalrymen are still in a disorganized pursuit of them. Forrest, as always, sees an opportunity for a sudden and unexpected attack and orders his men to charge the Yankees in columns of four with six-shooters blazing. When the bluecoats finally manage to repulse the attack, in what Wilson calls a "gallant fight," Forrest circles the enemy and rides to join Roddey's command. At nightfall, as the fighting comes to an end, Forrest goes into camp, sixteen miles south of Montevallo near the town of Randolph.[84]

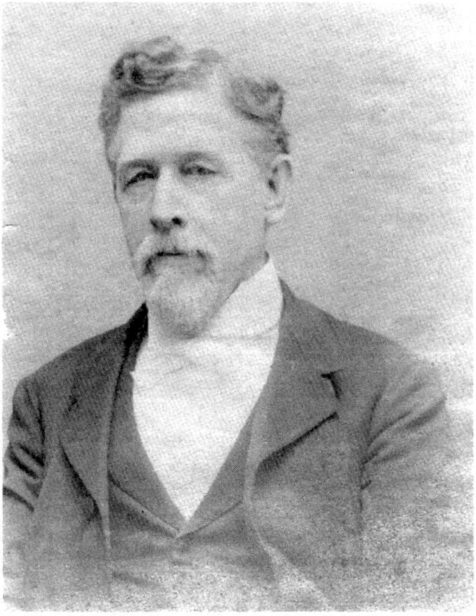

Confederate general Philip D. Roddey. *Courtesy Alabama Department of Archives and History, Montgomery, Alabama.*

During the night of March 31, Bedford Forrest's mind is clouded with worry. He still does not have his cavalry consolidated for a defense, and Wilson is driving him back with such ease that the Yankees will soon have an open road to Selma. If Jackson and Chalmers do not join him by tomorrow, April 1, he knows it will be too late to save Selma. But Forrest has a plan and is still hopeful it will come together. Only yesterday, he sent a courier to Red Jackson with a dispatch telling him of Wilson's position and directing him to "[f]ollow down after them, taking the road behind them from Montevallo." Meanwhile, Forrest is counting on Chalmers to cross the Cahaba River and join him near Plantersville. There, reinforced by Chalmers, he could make a stand, and Jackson, striking the Yankees from the rear, would place Wilson in a vice where he could be defeated. If the plan can come to fruition, as Forrest hopes, it is destined to be, in the opinion of one historian, "[o]ne of the greatest cavalry battles of the war"—or, as one of his soldiers predicts, "[t]he cavalry battle of the ages."[85]

But Forrest's plan of attack, though brilliant, will require good luck and lots of it. Instead, he will become the victim of a great deal of bad luck. The courier carrying the dispatch to Jackson, together with other important papers, is captured by one of Wilson's cavalrymen early on the morning of April 1. Unknown to Forrest, Jackson never gets the message and is still floundering on the other side of the Cahaba River, thanks to the efforts of Croxton in distracting him and to Wilson for sending one of McCook's brigades to destroy the Cahaba Bridge at Centerville. Finally, and probably worst of all, it seems that Chalmers is twenty miles away, moving in the opposite direction he had just been ordered to go on the night of March 31. Forrest is furious when he receives word from Chalmers that he would not be able to reach him by April 1 as a result of encountering so many obstacles. Forrest, now in a seething rage, sends couriers galloping back to his division commander, informing him of the desperate circumstances and telling him to reverse his direction and move quickly to the Randolph-Plantersville Road, leaving his artillery behind if that would enable him to move faster. Given Chalmers's usual reliability and promptness in previous situations such as this, his failure to reach Forrest in time seems inconceivable. After the war, in an address to the Southern Historical Society, Chalmers will contend that he had been delayed because of conflicting orders between Forrest and Richard Taylor and because he could not get across the Ochmulgee Swamp, claiming, "It was utterly impassable to the artillery." But Taylor, in his postwar memoirs, sees it differently. "The Federal commander…threw out false signals," he notes, adding that "two of [Forrest's] brigadiers permitted themselves to be deceived by reports of the enemy's movements."[86]

The only bit of good fortune Forrest finds on this April Fool's Day of 1865 comes quite by accident in the person of a thirty-year-old cavalryman named Frank Armstrong, who commands one of Chalmers's brigades. Armstrong and his brigade are some five miles north of Chalmers and the rest of the division when a courier comes galloping through their lines with a dispatch from Forrest to Chalmers. Reading the message, Armstrong immediately realizes the urgency of it and sends the courier on to Chalmers, along with his own comment that given their commander's precarious situation, "[he] would march to Forrest on his own responsibility" without waiting to receive orders from Chalmers. This he does, but not before spending five hours fighting his way through the mile-wide Ochmulgee Swamp, finally joining Forrest at about dusk on April 1. Unfortunately, just as Chalmers has already found out, Armstrong learns they cannot get their artillery or wagons through the boggy swamp and are forced to leave them behind. Much to everyone's regret, as one of his officers remembers, all of those essentials left behind "[we] were not to see again."[87]

To be sure, Harry Wilson's mood is a good one. After intercepting Forrest's dispatches, he knows the exact location of every brigade under his command, what his plans are and, most of all, what he must do. "If I could force the marching and the fighting with sufficient rapidity and vigor, I should have the game entirely in my hands," boasts Wilson. It's now apparent to the young general that there is a good possibility that it will be him, not Forrest, to strike "first with the most." For this, he is understandably proud to have "anticipated Forrest in his own game." At the same time, he knows that the man is a formidable opponent, and as George Thomas reminded one of his officers in a dispatch dated only yesterday, "[he] is, as you know, a tricky fellow." Wilson, though, believes he will be successful. "I determined to allow him no rest, but to overwhelm him if possible on the road, and failing in that, to drive him inside the works of Selma as soon as possible." Fortune, too, has smiled on Wilson, and he must take advantage of it, causing him to philosophically remark, "War is full of vicissitudes and Forrest is now in the midst of them."[88]

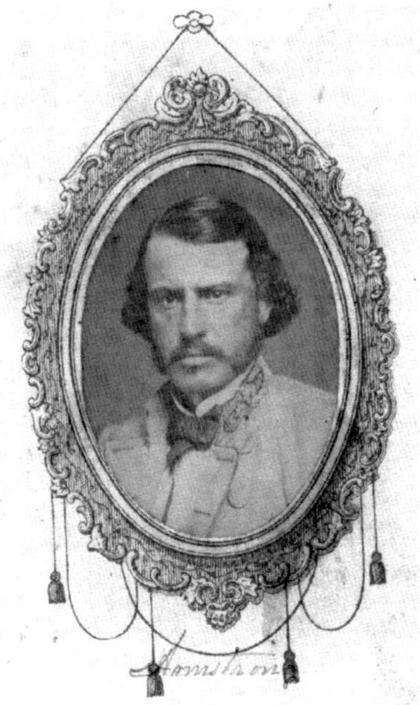

Confederate general Frank Armstrong. *Courtesy Alabama Department of Archives and History, Montgomery, Alabama.*

Indeed, the winds of war are not favorable for Forrest as the sounds of gunfire resume on the morning of April 1, signaling a running skirmish between the two sides that will continue for a distance of twenty-five miles. In the face of such weak resistance, Wilson kicks off the all-day affair by pushing two divisions forward: Emory Upton's division, numbering 3,900, moves south down the Old Maplesville Road, while the stronger division of Eli Long, with 5,127 horsemen, continues on a parallel course, pressing ahead down the main Selma Road and following the tracks of the Alabama and Tennessee River Railroad. Trailing behind them in support of Long is Edward McCook's partial division. Knowing that such a large force of cavalry would be impossible to defeat with his small force, Forrest is willing to trade geography for time, hoping he can delay their progress long enough for Chalmers and Jackson to arrive. Thus, most of this day, like yesterday, is spent in small, hit-and-run firefights beginning at a point just below the town of Randolph to Plantersville, which is only nineteen miles north of Selma.[89]

During this day, Forrest learns that he will not be reinforced by Chalmers or Jackson. As Wilson aptly points out, "There was nothing left him but to curse and fight." And so he will, deciding to make a stand about six miles north of Plantersville near Ebenezer Church. Here, the ground is naturally strong for a defensive stand, hilly and wooded, cut by ravines, flanked by creeks and ideal for artillery since it overlooks the point where the Selma and Old Maplesville roads converge. On this mile-long line, he places Dan Adam's untested militia on the right, at the eastern end, anchored by Mulberry Creek. The center, running along the north bank of Bogler's Creek, is occupied by Roddey's veteran division and the artillery, while the left is protected by Edward Crossland's three hundred Kentucky cavalrymen, perched on a wooded ridge. Altogether they number no more than two thousand and are facing a force five times that figure. To strengthen his position, Forrest orders rail and log barricades erected and has six pieces of artillery rolled to commanding points along the line, frowning down on the two approaching roads. With the artillery and behind the center stands Forrest, his escort and two hundred men of Armstrong's brigade.[90]

Out in front of the main line, Forrest has positioned a skirmish line, and here, at about 4:00 p.m., those soldiers see clouds of dust in the distance, moving down the Selma Road. Shrouded in the dust is the leading regiment of Long's division, the Seventy-Second Indiana Mounted Infantry. As the men approach within range, the advance gray line opens fire. Dismounting on Long's orders, the Hoosiers push forward through the pines bordering the road, delivering a blistering fire as they move. The Spencer repeating rifles prove too much for the Rebels' first line of defense. As might be expected, the line is quickly broken, and the panicked skirmishers rush pell-mell back into Forrest's main line.[91]

About this same time, the rattling sounds of gunfire are heard at the Dungan family home, which stands in the vicinity of Bogler's Creek near the battlefield-to-be. The father, Hall Dungan, a former Confederate soldier, is home from the war and permanently crippled by a wound to the arm. He and a female servant named Mal hastily grab as many provisions and valuables as they can carry and lead the children into the thick piney woods for shelter and concealment from what they rightly believe to be the approaching storm of battle. But Mrs. Dungan and her teenaged daughter, Mattie, insist on remaining behind, hoping they can somehow save their home from being destroyed and believing they could "encourage the Southern soldiers to stand by their guns."[92]

The sight of the retreating Rebel skirmishers leads Union general Eli Long to believe that this resistance is just another small force sent out by Forrest to delay his column with a hit-and-run ploy. Unaware that Forrest

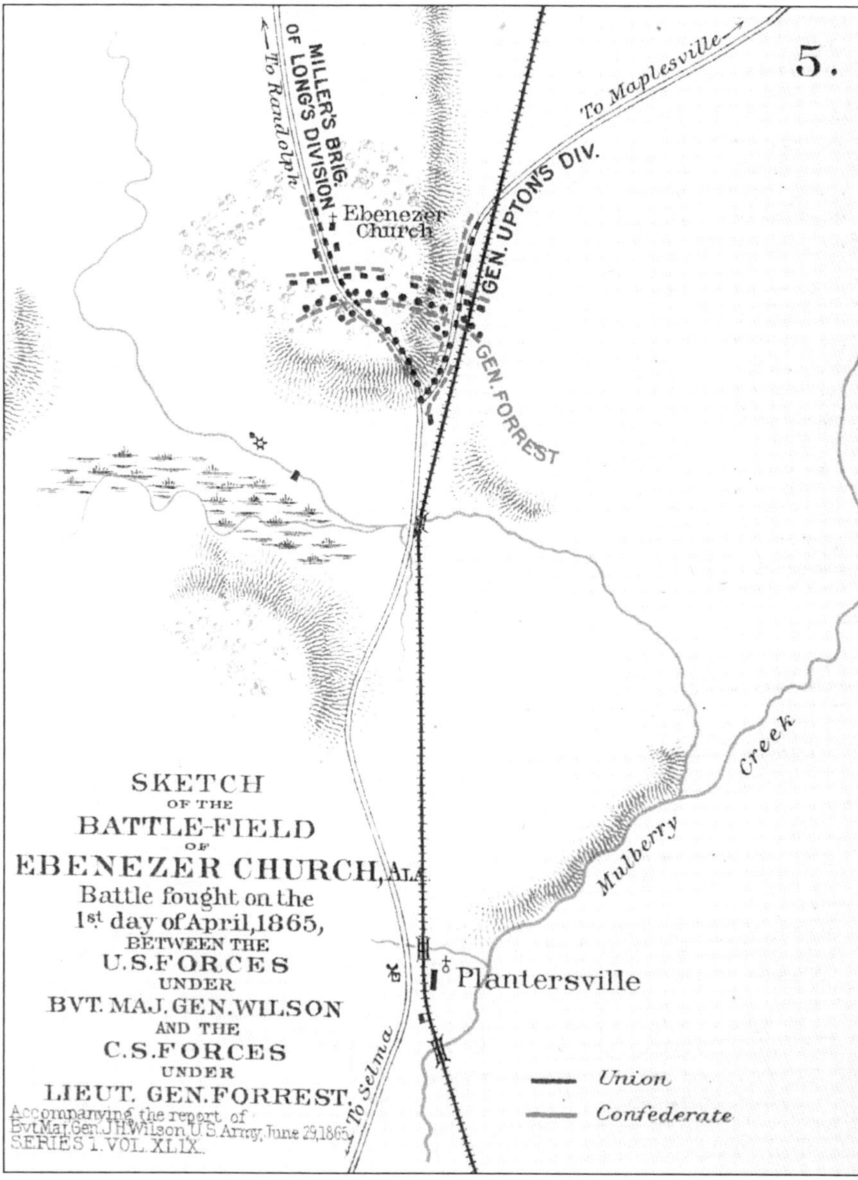

Map of the Battle of Ebenezer Church. *Courtesy the Texas Collection, Baylor University, Waco, Texas.*

has established a stronger defensive line ahead, Long orders Lieutenant Colonel Frank White to make a saber charge with four companies of the Seventeenth Indiana Mounted Infantry. Although such a charge against a prepared position would ordinarily be considered rash, Long feels that White will have no problem driving off what he thinks is only a handful of Rebels. Besides, according to Wilson's memoirs, "[Frank White] would have been a full match for Forrest himself had they met." Indeed, it would be a clash of titans, as Wilson goes on to describe White as "a berserker of the Norsemen breed, broad shouldered, deep-chested, long-limbed, over six feet tall, and bearded like a pard." But fate has other plans.[93]

Forrest, mounted on his huge horse, King Phillip, watches beside an artillery battery as the Yankee horsemen approach. "A cloud of dust was seen up the road, and a heavy column of Federals at full gallop with drawn sabers glistening in the sunlight came towards us," recalls a captain in Forrest's escort. Forrest then turns toward his escort and the two companies of Kentuckians behind him. He orders them to draw their revolvers, one in each hand, and as soon as the oncoming Yankees reach the Confederate line, they are to charge into them, firing at close range.[94]

Momentarily, the four Indiana saber companies punch through the Rebel line and begin slashing their way toward a four-gun artillery battery and Forrest's escort. In the gunfire, screams and confusion, one Federal soldier's horse goes berserk and becomes unmanageable. Man and beast crash into the carriage of one of the cannons with a force of impact so violent that it knocks a wheel from the gun's axle, collapsing the cannon and killing the horse. The stunned rider, sprawling on the ground, is immediately killed by a blow to the head from a rammer staff swung by a Rebel cannoneer.[95]

Over the din of battle, Forrest yells for his horsemen to charge. Riders tear forward, each one jockeying for the lead. But no one actually gets it in the short distance they have to go before a mass of horseflesh slams murderously into the lead squadron of the Yankee column. Now the sounds of thundering hooves give way to the gruesome sounds of battle, with men cursing, horses snorting, sabers clashing and pistol fire filling the air. The ensuing struggle soon becomes one of the most vicious hand-to-hand fights ever experienced between cavalry soldiers during this war.

Both sides are caught up in a maelstrom of whirling dust, gun smoke and spinning, half-ton horses. "The conflict was now terrible," remembers a Rebel cavalryman, "Every one of us, the general, staff, and escort, were surrounded by the Federals, and it seemed as if it was…every man for himself." Because the Union soldiers are using sabers instead of the six-shooters in the hands of Forrest's men, their losses are mounting faster. But through the smoke, Union captain James Taylor spots the headquarters flag of Forrest and leads a group of Indiana soldiers toward the prize. Without warning, "I saw General Forrest surrounded by six Federals at one time, and they were all slashing at him," recalls Lieutenant George Cowan. "One of them struck one of his pistols and knocked it from his hand." Apparently, Taylor and his soldiers recognize Forrest as an officer of high rank, judging from the observation of one Confederate staff officer: "It seemed as if those fellows were intent on killing the general." Captain Taylor then joins the attack, spurring his horse closer to Forrest, who is forced to throw up an arm to shield himself from the saber blows. Phil Dodd, only a private, is near and sees his general's dilemma. He shoots one of the assailants, enabling Forrest enough space to draw his other pistol and kill Captain Taylor. Finally, another member of Forrest's escort, Lieutenant John Eaton, fires on the last remaining attacker, dropping him dead from his saddle.[96]

Forrest, together with his escort and the Kentuckians, have beaten back the Indiana attack. The Yankee Hoosiers succeed in cutting their way out and escaping through the woods back to their lines. Among them is their commander, Lieutenant Colonel Frank White, whom Wilson thought to be "in the flower of his strength" and "a full match for Forrest." But the two did not meet. More than once, White, like Forrest, found himself completely surrounded by the enemy, but as Wilson later remarks, "His life seemed to be charmed and he fought his way out with but little injury."[97]

Hardly has White's saber charge been turned back than Emory Upton's division appears on the Old Maplesville Road. Staring at the situation in front of him, Upton immediately orders Andrew Alexander, commanding his leading brigade, to move into the battle. They strike the right of the Confederate line, where Dan Adams and his militia are positioned behind a rail fence with a battery of two guns. At the same time, Eli Long orders a fresh line of troops to advance up the Selma Road. Adams's untested militia quickly collapses under the weight of Upton's attack, causing Forrest to be flanked and caught in a crossfire between Upton and Long. Whatever hopes Forrest may have had for an orderly retreat now disappear, along with three of his cannons and three hundred of his men, who are taken prisoner. He makes his own escape by spurring King Phillip to jump completely over a gun carriage and carry him to safety. Then Forrest and the remainder of his command retreat rapidly down the Selma Road to the town of Plantersville, nineteen miles north of Selma, where they make camp for the night. The retreat is clearly a confused and disorderly rout, as one of the pursuing

Iowa cavalrymen later remembers, "The road was strewn with guns, belts, cartridge boxes, coats and hats."[98]

Although there is no official count of Confederate killed and wounded, most of Forrest's losses are clearly the result of men captured and missing. Wilson's victory has come at a cost of twelve dead and forty wounded, which is not a very significant number, considering the ferocity of the fight. Thinking back on it years later, a Union officer tells of the remote region the battle was fought in and explains how it was named: "A little meeting house, hitherto unnoticed, cropped out from the midst of the timber. Its people had christened it Ebenezer, and, as the fight was nearest this as any known place, the triumph went down among the annals as The Battle of Ebenezer Church."[99]

Also left standing is the Dungan family home. Watching the battle as it "waxed hot" and seeing Forrest's lines beginning to break, the mother and daughter become terrified. Fleeing the house, they take refuge in a nearby swamp. Now, as the sounds of battle fade into silence, they are anxious to see if their home is still standing but fearful the bluecoats might fire on them when they emerge from the swamp. Mattie, the resourceful daughter, tears a square of white cloth from her petticoat, attaches it to a cornstalk to improvise a flag of truce and bravely leads her mother to their home. Approaching the house, they see it still stands but is already being used as a Union hospital. Once inside, the sight turns ghastly as they find their home "filled with dead and dying Yankees, many of whom were buried in a trench in their yard."[100]

Despite his wounds and a day spent constantly fighting without rest over a distance of twenty-five miles, Forrest leaves camp and devotes the night of April 1 to searching the countryside for his missing troops. Many of them have been separated from the main body during the confusing afternoon retreat, and he knows he will need every man he can collect by tomorrow. Early in the evening, Frank Armstrong's brigade, numbering 1,432 horsemen, arrives. Welcomed as they are, Forrest knows, even with the added strength of this brigade, that he will not have enough troops to hold off Wilson's advance. By tomorrow, he will have no choice except to fall back into the defensive works of Selma.

A few miles away in the Union camp, fortune, once again, smiles on Harry Wilson. Scarcely has he finished celebrating his victory at Ebenezer Church than Emory Upton personally brings him a prisoner. The man's name is Milligan, an English engineer who has been employed by the Confederates to design the fortifications in Selma but has now peacefully surrendered to Upton. "It did not take long to learn he was exactly the man we needed," notes Wilson. At Upton's request, the engineer prepares a detailed sketch of all the fortifications, stockades, entrenchments and gun emplacements in the city. Wilson and Upton then spend an anxious night studying the sketch of what seems to them to be a masterfully constructed bastion. "It was evident," reflects Wilson, "that we were confronted by a mighty serious problem."[101]

Chapter 6

THE QUEEN CITY

The city of Selma, christened the "Queen City of the Black Belt" during its booming antebellum years, is situated in Dallas County on a high plateau overlooking the north bank of the Alabama River, one hundred feet above its ordinary stage. Most agree with one resident who describes it as an "exquisitely lovely, peaceful little city, with its broad streets, over-arching trees, beautiful homes and flowing river." Like the state's capital, Montgomery, Selma lies within the fertile region of Alabama's Black Belt, which originally took its name from the rich, black topsoil that gave rise to the area's numerous cotton plantations. But with the growing demand for agricultural workers, who were predominately black slaves, the name "Black Belt" took on an additional meaning during the nineteenth century. Given the land's natural capacity to produce abundant crops, it's not surprising that the Confederate government established a commissary department in the city for the distribution of meat, grain, fodder and other agricultural products to the Southern armies.[102]

And yet, Selma itself is largely an industrial and geographic product of the war. Within the city, there is every kind of war materiel manufactory, making everything from "a horse shoe nail to cannon carriages." Foundries, rolling mills, ironworks, machine shops, car shops, cotton and woolen mills and the huge naval works are spread over the town and its environs. Some are private, but most are government owned or controlled, with numerous factories covering some fifty acres and employing more than six thousand people. Next to the Tredegar Iron Works in Richmond, Selma has become

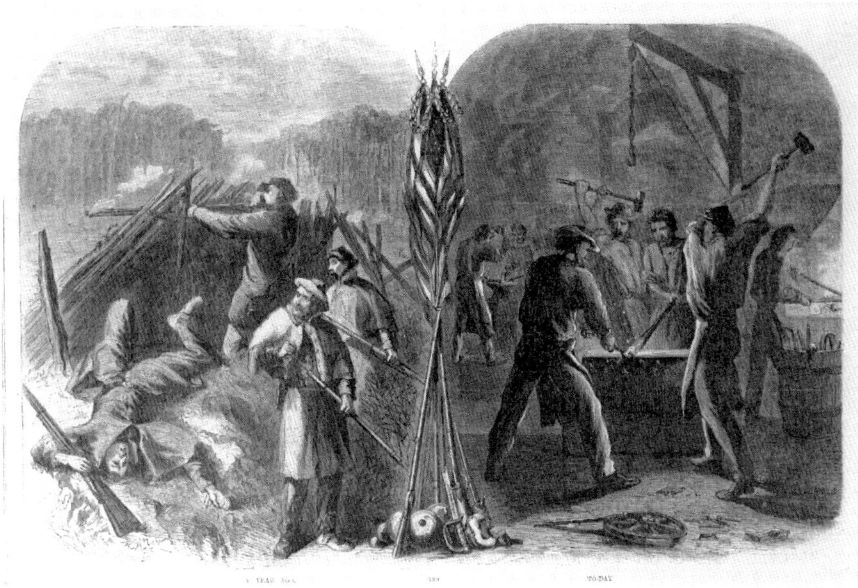

An illustration from *Frank Leslie's Illustrated Newspaper* depicting the importance of ironworking to the war effort. *Courtesy Library of Congress.*

the most important manufacturing center in the Confederate states. What's more, it's location in Central Alabama, the heart of the Confederacy, not only keeps it safe from the destruction of the battles raging throughout the South but also gives it an excellent geographic position to distribute its wares in any direction. In 1860, the population was listed as 3,177, but during the war years, the number of inhabitants explodes, with an estimated 10,000 workers swarming into the city in search of employment in government plants. As the war drags into its last year, the transient laborers are joined by flocks of refugees fleeing their war-ravaged homes to Selma and other cities lying within the Deep South. "Selma is full of refugees," complains Captain James Lynch in a letter to his wife. Lynch, clearly an educated man, has just been assigned to work as an engineer in the government's Nitre and Mining Bureau, and like so many others, he cannot find lodging in the congested town. "I borrowed a little cot and am sleeping in my office," he tells her.[103]

To its good fortune, Selma is served by railways, roads and a major waterway. Although they sustained some damage during the war, two railroads intersect within town, each with warehouses and factories lining their tracks. The Alabama and Tennessee River Railroad connects Selma with the vital mineral belt around Elyton and Montevallo, while the Alabama and Mississippi Railroad clatters its cars to Demopolis and then on to Meridian, Mississippi. Along with the railroads, six roads radiate from the city. Four of the roads run over a flat plain north of Selma. The main artery, known as the Range Line Road, runs due north to Plantersville, Randolph and Montevallo, the same route along which Wilson has been pushing Forrest. The Summerfield Road bears northwest from town, while another road goes directly west before bifurcating toward Marion and Cahaba. The Burnsville Road travels east across the low, swampy ground parallel to the Alabama River. On the south side of town, the Montgomery highway crosses the river and then follows it sixty miles to the capital. The Alabama River, of course, is a vital marine artery to carry Selma's goods to Montgomery and Mobile. Taken in sum, by 1865 Selma is the center of a transportation network that binds together practically all that remains of the Confederacy east of the Mississippi River.[104]

Because Selma is so vital to the Confederacy's war effort, the government has naturally exercised rigorous efforts to protect it by encompassing the city in a hardy row of fortifications. A line of works five miles long, shaped

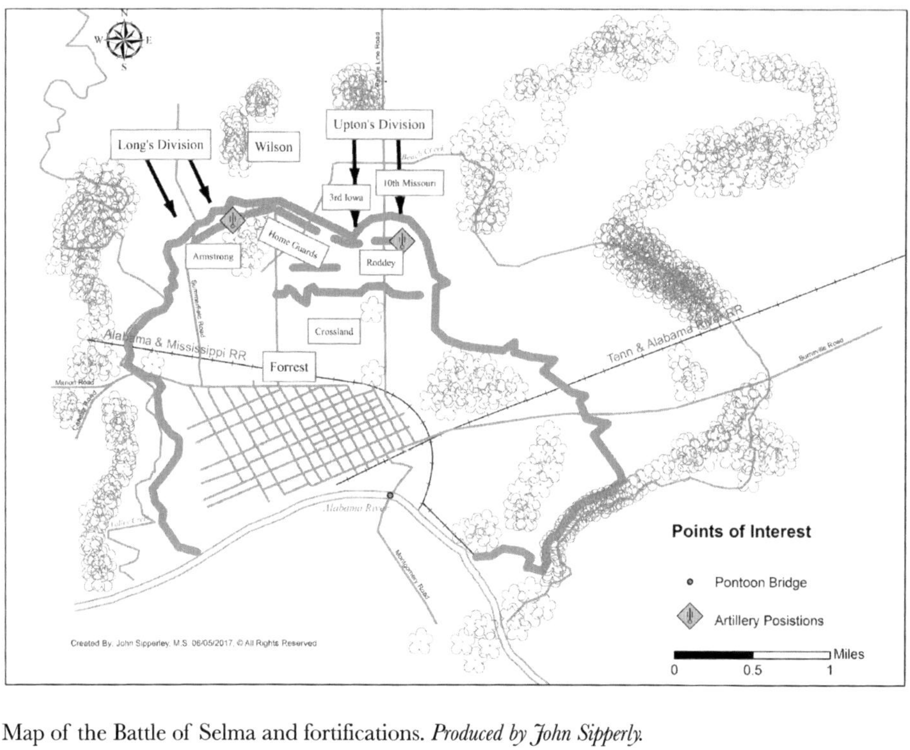

Map of the Battle of Selma and fortifications. *Produced by John Sipperly.*

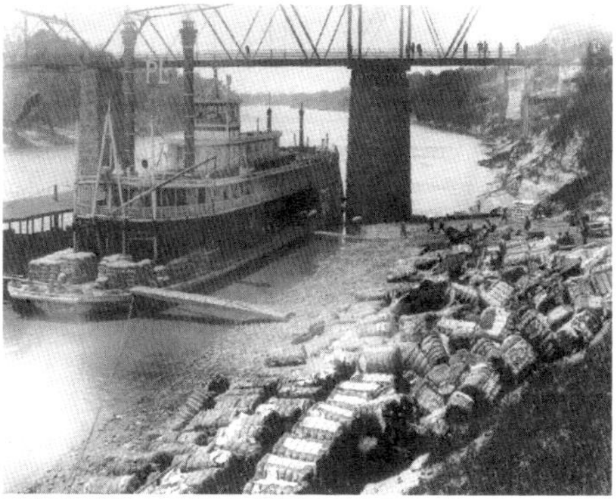

Postwar photograph of the steamer *City of Mobile* docked at wharf on the Alabama River at Selma. *Courtesy Alabama Department of Archives and History, Montgomery, Alabama.*

like a horseshoe, girdles the town. These works, constructed chiefly by slave labor, begin just west of Selma at the point where Valley Creek empties into the Alabama River and then meander north, east and south in a semicircle all the way to the mouth of Beech Creek. Along the way are menacing stockades and rifle pits. At the point where the line begins to veer northeast, near the Summerfield road, the fortifications become more impressive. Here an earthen parapet has been built, eight feet tall and eight feet thick at the base, with a water-filled ditch four feet wide and five feet deep lying in front of it. And beyond the ditch, sharpened posts, five feet long, have been planted in the ground to discourage an advance of the enemy. East of the Range Line Road and on to the river, the line resumes its less formidable character, employing only the rifle pits and stockades. Here and there, throughout the works, stand four forts, with artillery mounted to threaten a cleared killing ground in every direction. The defensive line to the south is, of course, the mighty Alabama River, a natural barrier. But if an attack is made, it will surely come from the open country lying north of the city, notwithstanding the fact that this is the segment with the strongest fortifications.[105]

On April 1, the same day Forrest is trying to stave off Wilson and his raiders at Ebenezer Church, Selma is bustling in a state of uproar and confusion. Mrs. C.E. Landis has just returned by train from a lengthy visit to Marion when she hears the news that a large force of Yankee cavalry is fast approaching the city. "I learned that for over a week everything which could be gotten out of the city had been shipped to other points, and everyone who could possibly get away had left the city." Most, however, have chosen to remain in their homes and hope for the best. What else could they do? In session is a council of war made up of civilian and military authorities, including Mayor John H. Henry, General Dan Adams and General Richard Taylor, who has rushed from Meridian to Selma upon receiving news of the emergency. Because Forrest has made it clear to these men that without Jackson and Chalmers there would be little chance of successfully defending the city, Mayor Henry is in favor of surrendering the place. But Taylor, commanding all troops in Alabama and Mississippi, has the final say and overrules him, insisting that "Selma itself would be defended at all costs." It's also likely that Forrest agrees with Taylor, regardless of his opinion that without the rest of his command there would be little chance of keeping Wilson from taking the city. In fact, Forrest has already announced his intentions to the citizens in a letter to the *Selma Evening Reporter*: "I am for fighting as long as there is a man left to fight with."[106]

Throughout the night of April 1, Forrest's tired and beaten men continue straggling into the city, a sight few of the citizens will ever forget. Seeing them only adds to the fear and tension of a people who have yet to experience the wrathful hand of war. Along with the disturbing sight of retreating soldiers come the sounds signaling an imminent danger. On the front porch of their home, Emily Ferguson and her family listen to "the rumble of the hand trucks and the splash as heavy items hit the water of the Alabama River." What they are hearing, of course, are the sounds of cannons plunging into the river, rolled there by teams of men under the command of George Peacock, superintendent of the naval gun foundry. There they will be buried in the black waters of the Alabama River to keep them from being seized by the Yankee raiders.[107]

On Sunday morning, April 2, Selma is in a state of wild confusion as Wilson's troops are near the threshold of the city—only nineteen miles away and moving closer. Down at the river, cannons are still being dumped, and cotton bales are stacked up on the docks, awaiting steamers for transport to Montgomery. Long trains of cars line the tracks, full of military equipment, bound for Demopolis. Horse-drawn wagons and carts laden with boxes and barrels clog the roadways leading west and south. Wandering in the streets are soldiers searching for their units. Mingling among them are civilians, gripping their valuables and searching for some means of escape. "I spent most of the morning standing out in front of our home weeping and wringing my hands in utter helplessness," remembers a very distraught Mrs. Landis. "Wounded soldiers had been passing our home at intervals for many hours. None of them were able to hold up their heads, but they were lying on their horses with feet dangling, their arms entwined around their necks, and heads resting in their horse manes. These soldiers were a part of Forrest's men… unfit for service from the long and fierce running fight."

Hundreds of miles away in Richmond, Jefferson Davis sits alone in his pew at St. Paul's Episcopal Church. He listens to the choir as it sings the hymn "Jesus, Lover of My Soul," and readies himself to receive communion. From the front of the church, a sexton slips down the aisle and touches the president on the shoulder, handing him a message. Opening it, he sees that it's a telegram from General Lee, telling him his lines have been broken and the capital would have to be evacuated immediately. As he quietly slips from the pew and walks out of the church, his face is rigid with lines of worry. Yet he does not know, because he cannot, that Selma, the vital war manufacturing center of the Deep South, is at this very moment facing the same fate as Richmond. It seems, then, that the entire Confederacy is tottering on the brink of collapse.[108]

At about ten o'clock this same morning, Forrest and his escort ride into Selma. Forrest goes directly to the Gee House, the city's best hotel, now serving as headquarters for his superior, Richard Taylor. Taylor recalls the moment: "Forrest appeared, horse and man covered with blood, and announced the enemy at his heels, and that I must move at once to escape capture." As the two continue to confer, Taylor becomes concerned as he studies the wounds Forrest received at Ebenezer Church. "I felt anxious for him," remembers Taylor, "but he said he was unhurt and would cut his way through as most of his men had done." Looking back on it, Taylor remarks, "There was nothing more to be done"—nothing, that is, except for him to try to escape. He recalls, though, that "capture seemed inevitable." There is, however, one small steam locomotive remaining in Selma that has been reserved for Taylor's escape, and he quickly boards it. "My engine started toward Meridian," he remembers, "and barely escaped."[109]

Forrest then goes about trying to organize a last-minute defense of the city. Even though the city has a strong, formidable line of defensive works, Forrest has nowhere near enough troops to properly man them. But Selma has a large population of citizens, workers and refugees, and Forrest, with little choice, will not hesitate to use them. No matter what their "calling or position" in life happens to be, every able-bodied male, Forrest orders, "[m]ust go into the works or into the river." Squads of armed men are sent from house to house, building to building, looking for men to press into service, sparing no one. Most of them, however, do not need to be coerced or forced, as they grab their shotguns, old flintlocks, pistols or anything that will

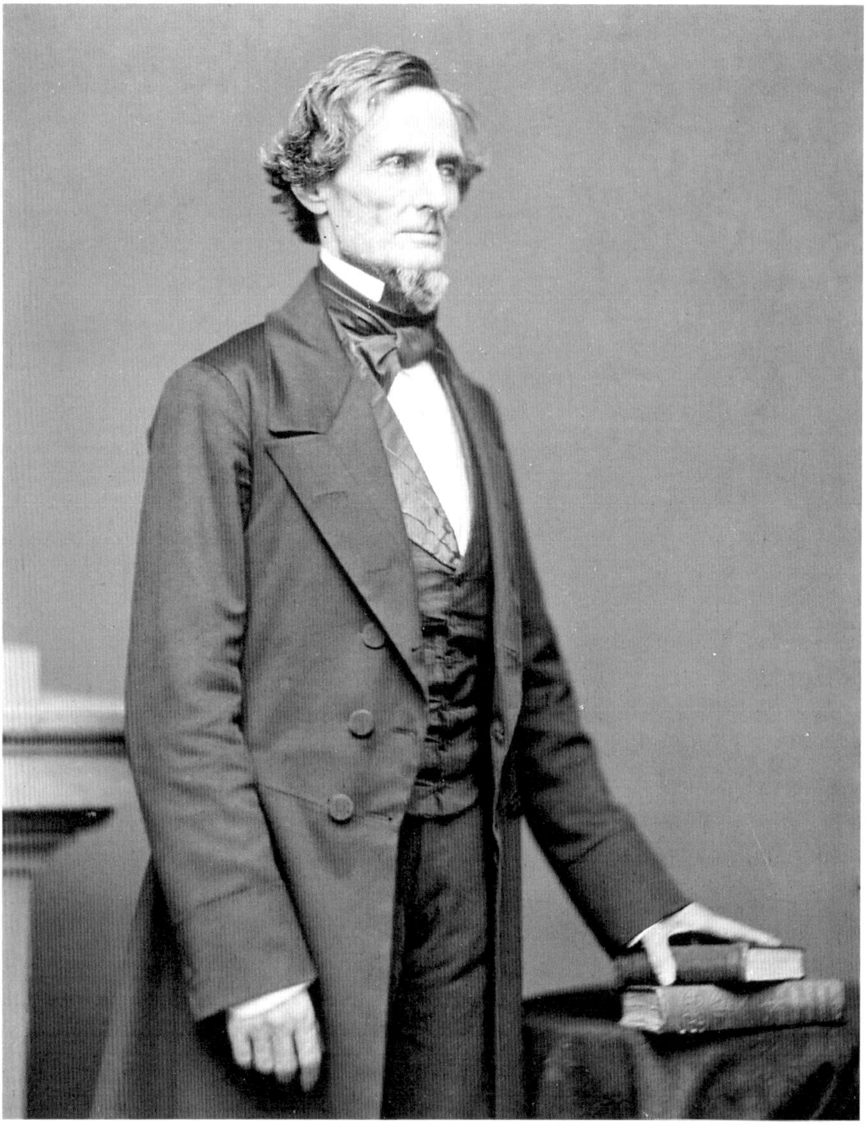

Confederate president Jefferson Davis. *Courtesy National Archives.*

fire a shot and rush to the fortifications. Lewis Riggs, newspaper owner and publisher, picks up his musket, leaves his office and goes with the others, as does Dr. Samuel Vaughan, who brings his thirteen-year-old son along. Even the Presbyterian minister, Reverend Small, along with other "preachers of the gospel took muskets and went into the trenches."

As one witness puts it, "Every man who could walk, every boy who could shoulder a musket, returned soldiers, refugees, workmen from the shops, took their appointed places in the defenses, armed and equipped in a manner unknown in civilized modern warfare." But they bear little resemblance to a true fighting force—say, the Spartans who defended Thermopylae or, for that matter, any trained soldiers. In sum, they're a motley collection of poorly armed, undrilled civilians posing as soldiers. Although there is no accurate count of this "rough looking squad," as one bystander describes them, a fair estimate would number somewhere between 1,800 and 2,000. They take their place in the works alongside Armstrong's veteran Mississippi brigade, five regiments of Alabamians under Roddey, Crossland's three Kentucky regiments and, of course, Forrest's escort. Taken together, their total strength probably does not exceed 4,000. But regardless of the number, the fortified line is so long that to cover it the men are standing at intervals of six to ten feet, a distance too far apart to effectively hold off a Federal force as strong as Wilson's.[110]

In town, the women, children and elderly who have remained behind are by no means idle in preparing for the enemy's arrival. Selma—if compared to the rest of the beaten South in 1865—is a rich place, and many of its citizens are desperate to protect their valuables from being pillaged. Mrs. Francis Hobbs, whose husband is a jeweler but is now off with the army, spends the hours prior to the attack sewing valuable pieces of jewelry into her petticoat, while down the street, the local banker, Washington Smith, is busy hollowing out one of the columns of his home to hide the funds of the Bank of Selma. Behind the drugstore at the corner of Furnish and Broad Streets, druggist Lewis Bayne is burying bottles of medicine. And P.J. Weaver, an old man who has no intention of parting with his money, is digging up his property with the help of his slave, Jack, to inter his gold and silver. Not everyone, however, is concerned only with the safety of their personal wealth. At the hospital, known as the Old Institute, women and girls, such as Mary Lavandar, use the time before the battle to gather medical supplies and tear rags and sheets into bandages for the wounded they know will come. Out in the streets, some local merchants, in one final precaution, are piling barrels of whiskey to be destroyed, fearful of the Yankee's behavior should they find and consume it.[111]

All morning, since reveille, Harry Wilson has spent preparing for the attack. Horses, arms, ammunition and other equipment have all been "well looked after." Having spent hours during the night planning and consulting with Emory Upton, Wilson rides off to meet with another division commander, Eli Long. Since their divisions will be spearheading the attack, he wants to make sure they understand every detail of the operation. Wilson also includes brigade and regimental officers in his instructions, especially the Irish colonel Robert Minty and Colonel Abram Miller, both of whom will play an important role in the attack. "I showed them the Englishman's sketch," he writes later, "explaining every detail…the works and their ditches, the stockades, the open ground, the small creeks or runs, the woods and the swamps outside, and pointed out every conceivable difficulty." He also explains that the works must be taken and that failure is not an option. "There was not an officer that did not understand this," recalls Wilson, who then gives them a "word of encouragement."[112]

Shortly after three o'clock in the afternoon, Wilson's cavalry comes within sight of the city. "Nine thousand sabers, with two field batteries…every man a veteran," Wilson recounts as he remembers their vast presence on the field. Following the plan, Long's division moves slightly west to the Summerfield Road, while Upton's division continues moving on the Plantersville or Range Line Road, as it's called when it nears Selma. Wilson now has a good view of the fortifications as he looks down from a ridge north of town. Wondering about the accuracy of Millington's sketch, he spurs his horse along the length of the ridge, studying the Rebel lines. "To my gratification," says the Federal commander, "[I] found it to be surprisingly accurate." Seeing no reason to change his battle plan, he sends word to his officers that the attack will proceed at the sound of the signal gun.[113]

About six hundred yards from Selma's defenses, Upton and Long halt their long columns just out of range of the Rebel cannons that have begun throwing shells their way. The Union commanders then order their men to dismount and form into a single line of attack that stretches across both roads approaching the city. Sporadic picket fire from skirmishers then starts popping and mingling with the exchange of desultory artillery fire between the Chicago Board of Trade Battery and the big guns in the Rebel forts. On both sides, men are wondering how a Yankee, or anyone else, could survive charging a distance of several hundred yards over such open ground. Out on the Range Line Road, a Missouri officer, lying on the ground among his men, watches and waits for the order to attack. "The cannon spoke plainly all along the whole line of works & the rattling of small arms became quite lively, but I knew all this was nothing but play, & that before we could reach the city the very earth would tremble."[114]

Somewhere between the hours of four and five o'clock in the afternoon, while waiting for the attack to begin, a glitch is thrown into Wilson's prearranged battle plans. Eli Long's division on the Summerfield Road is attacked in the rear by "a force of rebel cavalry estimated from 500 to 1,000 men." In the safety of the rear, of course, is where Long's supply trains are located, and fortunately he has had the foresight to expect something like this. Thus, he has already deployed a few regiments to protect the rear of his division from any such attack, and the Rebel charge is easily repulsed. Long rightly suspects that the Rebels behind him are the advance elements of Chalmers's division coming to the aid of Forrest. If so, he knows there will be more on the way. Now he begins to fret over the tormenting thought of Chalmers launching a full-blown attack on his rear before he can set his frontal attack in motion. This prods him into ordering his division forward immediately, without waiting for orders from Wilson or the planned signal to attack. But given the circumstances, Wilson will later congratulate the division commander for his "admirable judgment" and praise his initiative as "fully justified."[115]

While the sun is beginning to sink beneath the rolling hills in front of Selma, Miss Mattie Harrell stands alone with her invalid mother and two younger children. Her father has just rushed off to help man the breastworks. Now as she stares up the road leading to the first line of the city's defenses she sees "the dark cloud of blue coats which shortly formed on the horizon growing more ominous." Even closer, out in the breastworks, Frank Montgomery, commanding the First Mississippi Regiment of Armstrong's brigade, describes the same spectacle. "While we were all looking—the sun was nearly down—a long, dark line of men appeared on the brow of the ridge; they moved slowly forward for a while, and then broke into a cheer and charged."[116]

Waiting for the Yankees' approach, Mississippian Frank Montgomery comes to a prophetic conclusion. "I make no doubt," he says, "Forrest was either cursing Chalmers for not coming up, or praying that he might come in the night." Actually, Montgomery's prognosis is generally accurate. Forrest, at this moment, is with Dan Adams in the telegraph office, frantically trying to get a last-minute message to Chalmers. The two men are interrupted when an excited young black boy bounds through the door and frantically announces, "The Yankees is cum."[117]

Chapter 7

The Horrors of War

At almost the same time the attack of Long's division gets underway on the Union right, Upton, "hearing the noise of battle to his right…waited for neither signal nor orders" and orders his men to begin wading through the swamp and brush in their immediate front until they are swarming south on the Range Line Road toward that part of the line defended by Roddey's cavalry, the Home Guards and what will prove to be a hopeless collection of civilians. One of Upton's troopers, remembering the charge, describes it in a vivid rendition: "Volley followed volley; the long rattle of our Spencers, and the reply by our batteries to the incessant heavy booming of guns from the forts. With a cheer, our boys charge dismounted across the fields and swamps, over rifle pits and embankments, over trenches and palisades, up through the battery smoke, on to the parapet, yelling like devils."[118]

But the real challenge lies in front of Long's troops coming down the Summerfield Road. This part of the Confederate line is defended by Frank Armstrong and his 1,500 doughty Mississippians. They are, by far, the best Forrest has to offer since the rest of his regulars could not—for reasons Old Bedford has yet to understand—join him in the defense of Selma. Frank Montgomery, commanding the left of Armstrong's line, watches Long's troops as they draw closer, numbering what he believes to be at least three thousand men. "I hastened to my place in line," recalls the Mississippian, "and was barely in time to caution the men not to fire till I gave the word." But some of the more edgy men do not wait for his

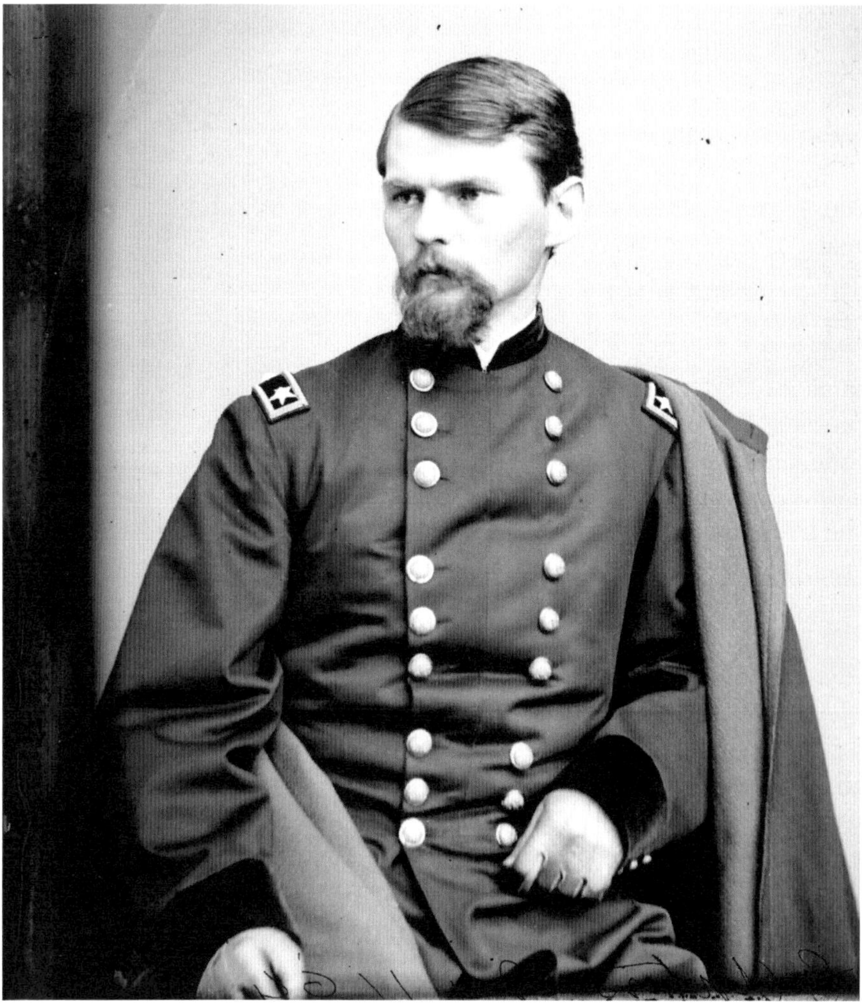

Union division commander General Emory Upton. *Courtesy Library of Congress.*

order and, in Montgomery's opinion, begin firing too soon. And yet, as the smoke drifts away and the enemy nears, he admits, "I could plainly see the deadly effects of our fire."[119]

The effects are "deadly" indeed. The Mississippi riflemen have taken a heavy toll on the charging Federals. But the first wave of Long's men has reached the palisade and manages to squirm its way through or around the sharpened wooden stakes and into the deep ravine in front of the fortifications. Montgomery sees the men in his immediate front, where they have "gotten to the ravine and crowding into it for protection from our fire." Many of them are now only twenty feet from the breastworks when Montgomery goes to the top of the parapet and fires his pistol "five times into the struggling mass." While reloading, he hears "wild cheering to the right" and orders two of his companies to follow him around a salient in the line, where they discover that the right flank of their regiment is breaking apart. "I could see the enemy pouring over the works to the right, not a hundred yards away."[120]

The first man to reach the top of the works is Corporal John Booth, an Ohioan who, according to a soldier beside him, is "killed literally at the cannon's mouth, as a portion of his body was blown away just as he was entering the embrasure." Out in front of the breastworks, the division commander, General Eli Long, nearly meets the same fate as he's "stricken down…by a bullet which plowed through his scalp," producing a concussion and leaving his tongue paralyzed along with the right side of his face. With Long now reeling in confusion and unable to think clearly, the command falls to vibrant, blond Irishman Robert Minty, who continues pushing the division forward. Although he comes through unscathed, several of the regimental and brigade commanders are not so fortunate and are killed or wounded. Those officers may have avoided being shot had they not been mounted on horseback, high in the saddle, and making excellent targets of themselves. "In less time than it takes to tell it," Wilson remarks, when recounting Long's charge, "four officers and thirty-eight men were killed, while two hundred and seventy were wounded."[121]

While that was the worst of it, it was hardly the end of it. Notwithstanding the fact that Long's division has, in the gloating words of Major Beaumont, "swept over the defenses…like an avalanche," and the Stars and Stripes planted atop the works, courtesy of John Morgan, an Illinois sergeant, there are still Rebels fighting inside the fortifications. And now it's hand-to-hand, with muskets and rifles being swung like clubs. Rebel soldiers and their civilian conscripts find themselves under fire from the front and rear as bluecoats begin swarming on both sides of the breastworks. Those not shot down or captured begin scrambling through the smoke and confusion back toward town, where there is an inner line of defense. That line, however, has only been partially completed. Still, it is a much shorter one and more tenable for the small remaining force that is able to fight.[122]

"I knew that all was lost," laments Frank Montgomery. He and his fellow Mississippians are among the last in Armstrong's brigade to begin falling back to the inner line. Before they can do so, however, they realize they're being fired upon from the top of the works. "Seeing it impossible to get away," Montgomery knows he is facing a potential slaughter. Having already lost one-fourth of his men killed and wounded, and even more as prisoners, he makes the decision to surrender. "I gave the last order I ever gave during the war, and that was to the men to throw down their arms," he remembers. "In a moment a crowd of blue coats was around us."[123]

Just to the east, where the breastworks cross the Range Line Road, Upton's troops have already overpowered the defenders there, all made up of the Home Guard Militia and a mob of civilians. Mounted officers yell at the men scaling the works, "Go in boys, give them hell, we have the city, we are all right, give them hell." By the time Upton's men are into the works, the Rebel line is already broken. "The Rebels were seen skedaddling in all directions," notes one Union officer. Actually, the gap created by the fleeing militiamen was the primary cause for the desperate withdrawal of Forrest's veteran troops. Once the Yankees poured in, there was no choice for Armstrong and Roddey except to order their men to fall back to the second or interior line defended by Crossland's Kentuckians.[124]

Inside the breastworks, the divisions of Upton and Long are now poised to strike the inner line. But Harry Wilson wants the honors: "I felt it my duty to show myself on my most conspicuous horse with staff, escort, and red battle-flag in the thickest of the fight." Right away he summons the only mounted troops on the field, his escort detachment, the Fourth United States Cavalry, and orders the men to charge the Rebel interior line. "I promptly dismounted the horse I had been riding all day, sprang on my splendid gray gelding, Sheridan, and…bade them follow at the charge." Soon, Wilson's riders discover they are paying the price for their leader's quixotic desires. "All at once the whole top of the embankment was one sheet of fire, flame and smoke and the bullets fairly piped and screamed through the air," declares one of the horsemen. "The fort had all of a sudden become choked full of gray uniforms and bristling with muzzles of guns and bayonets." Wilson then hears one of the Rebel officers call out, "Shoot that man on the white horse." But they hit the horse instead. "My horse fell instantly with a bullet in his breast," recalls the general. "As he sank to the ground I threw myself from the saddle, but had hardly touched the ground before he was on his feet with his head high in the air and his eyes blazing as though they were balls of fire." Wilson's horse, Sheridan, will carry him through the rest of the battle and into the night, but the wound will prove to be mortal.[125]

Repulsed, Wilson and his horsemen fall back and re-form. By this time, the sky is melting from dusk to dark. A second charge is then organized, but this time, Wilson wisely adds the strength of two regiments from Upton's division as well as the artillery of the Chicago Board of Trade Battery, which is brought up so close it is "muzzle to muzzle with the enemy's guns on the inner entrenchments." The second attack immediately breaks the Rebel line, the last line of defense for the city of Selma. Forrest, knowing that further resistance would be useless, gives the order for the men to get to their horses and "escape as best they could." The sudden retreat, of course, creates a scene of wild confusion. "The city was in a turmoil," remembers one frightened resident. "All rushed to the front porches and street and saw riderless, foaming horses, wounded, tearing down the road in maddened terror, reins hanging loose, blankets slipping, going pell-mell down to the river."[126]

"I will never forget the horrors of that night," sighs Frank Montgomery, who together with 2,700 others, both soldier and civilian, are taken prisoner and marched to a stockade on the Alabama and Mississippi Railroad that, ironically, had formerly housed Federal prisoners. The number of Confederate soldiers and civilians killed is unknown, but among them are quite a few prominent citizens, including Reverend Small, who this same morning had preached a sermon at the Presbyterian church before going to the breastworks, and Lewis Riggs, the newspaper publisher, dead from a bullet wound to the stomach. Others fall into the missing category, their fates unknown, such as Miss Mattie Harrell's father, who never returns home after the fighting. Some, however, manage to get away in the darkness and confusion, running through the swamps or attempting to swim the Alabama River.[127]

Here and there, well into the night, small firefights continue breaking out. "Some of our men were shot from their saddles after entering the city," remembers one Iowa man, who describes the scene as "citizens scared, women and children screaming, excitement high everywhere." Those pockets of resistance that continue fighting only serve to infuriate the vengeful Union soldiers on a night one witness labels as "blood curdling." The chaos, coupled with the darkness and violence, makes it impossible for the Federal officers to control their troops. Companies and squads of men disintegrate into armed mobs, roaming the streets, pillaging and breaking into houses and stores. In the pandemonium, slaves escape their masters and join in the looting. To make matters worse, soldiers stumble upon the barrels of whiskey that the merchants apparently forgot (or the authorities did not have time to destroy). This, of course, only adds to the plundering and brutality. Innocent citizens begin to be victimized in the melee. And cruelty seeks out everyone, even

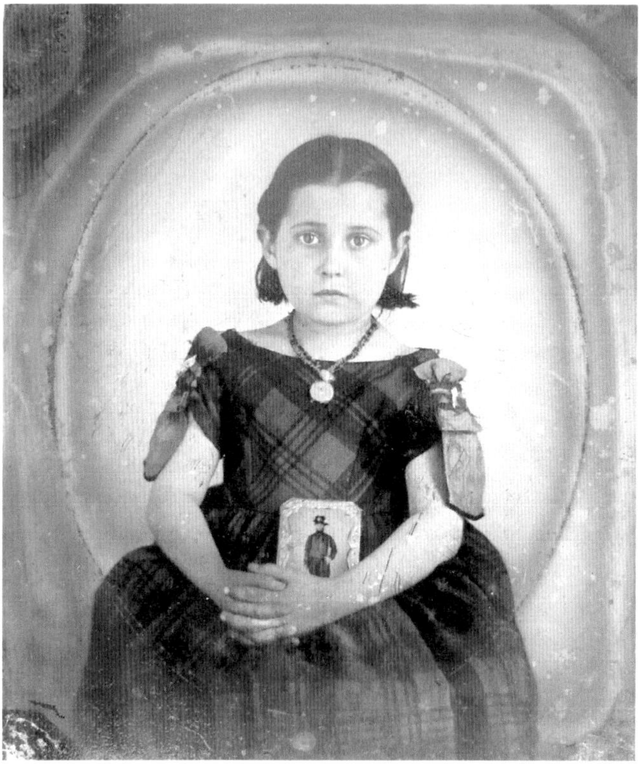

An unidentified girl in mourning, one of the many children left without a father during the Civil War. *Courtesy Library of Congress.*

older men, such as B.J. Duncan, who is pistol-whipped as his house is being ransacked, and Mr. Phil Weaver, "killed by some marauders while sitting on his back porch." Although there is no evidence of physical brutality toward women on this first night of occupation, Lewis Parsons, who later becomes governor of Alabama, claims, "Every woman was robbed of her watch, her earrings, her finger rings."[128]

At about ten o'clock in the evening, the first building begins to burn: a three-story structure at the corner of Water and Broad Streets. Supposedly, it was used, from time to time, as a guard house for Federal prisoners and thus, in revenge, is put to the torch by a soldier named Gibson, who had been held there. But whoever or whatever was responsible for setting the first fire nearly succeeds in destroying the city. From the corner building, the fires spread rapidly, roaring down Broad Street and consuming a full five blocks, including St. Paul's Episcopal Church. Farther away, near the river, the Central Cotton Warehouse goes up in flames. It was undoubtedly set by retreating Confederates to keep the cotton out of Federal hands and to carry out Richard Taylor's last orders before he left town. The warehouse fire, being near the arsenal, shoots missiles of burning embers into the barracks and ammunition houses until, according to a Federal officer, there are "shells exploding and flying in every direction." One diary entry for a Union officer on General Upton's staff reads: "Of all the nights of my experience, this is most like the horrors of war—a captured city burning at night, a victorious army advancing, and a demoralized one retreating....If there is a merciful God in the heavens, He must be looking down upon this scene in pity."[129]

Out on the Cahaba Road, miles away, the last of the military supply wagon trains from Selma rumbles toward safety. Traveling with the train is a number of Southern refugees who have fled the city at the first sounds of the guns. Among them is young Ethel Armes, who years later shares her memories of the glowing sky above Selma: "Under cover of the dark, a long wagon train retreated, loaded with quartermaster's and ordnance supplies—all that was saved for the Confederacy out of Selma....Hour after hour, mile after mile, the red glow sped like screaming shells after them. At midnight they halted at the Cahaba Ferry and even then—ten miles away—every bush and tree stood etched in sharp black lines against the flaming sky that told of the fall of Selma."[130]

Because of so many reported incidents of plundering, destruction, burning and other outrages committed by the Union troops, it would seem that the entire army is composed of lawless criminals. This, however, is not entirely true. Individually, most of the soldiers in both armies are generally decent men, although, as Frank Montgomery points out, "There were brutal men in both armies." But taken together, the good and the bad of both armies, they have become a hardened horde of men, calloused by war to the point that they hold a cynical disregard or indifference toward human suffering. Thus, when atrocities are committed against the enemy's soldiers and civilians, men who are otherwise virtuous often ignore it as nothing more than a byproduct of war. Some of them, bitter and vengeful over losses of their friends and comrades, become caught up in violent behavior they would normally find repugnant. And at times, such behavior becomes contagious, escalating from a few random acts of barbarity to many of the rank and file joining in the cruelty. In situations like this, officers are unable to maintain any semblance of discipline. Such is the case at Selma, epitomized when Mrs. C.E. Landis is chased from her home by drunken soldiers carousing in and out of her house in search of valuables. Out on the street, frantic and searching for someone in authority, she overhears one of her neighbors complaining to a Federal officer and asking if he would send someone to guard their homes. The officer replies, "Madam, if you find one man among these soldiers who is honorable enough to guard your home for the night, you are welcome, but I have no more control over these men than you have."[131]

There is, however, one man who can gain control over these soldiers: their commander, Harry Wilson. But even Wilson is unable to restore order until the early hours of the morning. Although he's not a man who advocates unnecessary violence or destruction of private property, he admits that there were indiscriminate acts of wickedness perpetrated against civilians. "Some of the marauders and desperadoes who always find [a] place in modern armies doubtless took part in plundering the stores and occasionally in breaking into private houses," he confesses, "but all such work was ruthlessly and promptly stopped as soon as it became known." Neither does the general believe in what will come to be known as "scorched earth" warfare against nonmilitary targets. Thus, when the fires begin raging in several places and endangering the town, Wilson sends out his provost guards to try to keep them from spreading. After the Episcopal church is burned down and the fire races toward the Presbyterian church, explicit orders come from Wilson: "No more churches burned." The guards manage to save that building, but despite any efforts to control them, most of the fires will continue to burn for the next two days.[132]

At some point in the early evening, Bedford Forrest makes his escape from the city. Riding with him is Frank Armstrong, whose troops have covered the retreat, and a considerable number of cavalrymen from various units, including Forrest's escort. Their getaway route is east of town, along the Burnsville Road, a roadway that they hope is unguarded and still open. But as they begin turning northward, galloping toward Plantersville, they collide with a detachment of Union horsemen, and Old Bedford, true to his promise to Taylor, is compelled to "cut his way through." It's here that another impulsive Yankee horseman makes the reckless decision to attack Forrest. And it's here, in hand-to-hand combat, that Forrest kills his thirtieth and last man of the war. The number of horses shot from under him, however, will remain at twenty-nine, as his favorite charger, King Phillip, survives the attack and the war.[133]

After the attack, Forrest and his escort continue picking their way along the dark highway until they hear cries of women coming from a house a short distance off the road. Forrest halts the escort and sends a detachment of men to investigate the disturbance. The troops surround the house and discover four Union soldiers, who are apparently either stragglers or deserters, rifling through their valuables and then attacking the women. Surprised, the intruders begin running from the house, loaded with plunder, but they're all killed or captured by the gray riders.

By some accounts, the outrage committed against these women excites the men of the escort into such a frenzy that they crave to punish other Union troops who might be engaging in such behavior. And that finally leads to another controversial incident in Forrest's career. Later in the evening, the Rebels capture a Union sentry from a nearby outpost. From their prisoner, they learn that a scouting detachment of Federal troops, about fifty strong from Wilson's escort, is now camping a short distance away at the farm of a man named Godwin. Whether or not Forrest believes the intentions of these Union men to be nefarious is unclear, but he orders an attack. What is clear, however, is that Lieutenant George Cowan and the escort, believing a night attack to be too hazardous to risk the general's life, refuse to make the attack unless Forrest remains a quarter-mile in the rear with the horse holders. And surprisingly, the man who is always eager for a fight agrees to stay out of it.

From this point, the facts surrounding the attack become contentious. In the aftermath of the incident, Union accounts maintain that Forrest and his men "charged on them in their sleep, and refusing to listen to their cries of surrender killed or wounded the entire party." Wilson, upon hearing the stories of what his soldiers are now proclaiming as a slaughter, attributes the cruel affair to Forrest's "ruthless temper" and feels that such incidents are becoming "far too frequent." Biographers of George Thomas even argue that Forrest himself was not only there but also the guilty perpetrator, claiming, "Forrest fell upon the party with the ferocity of a wild Indian, and killed every man of it." But the Confederate version differs, insisting that Forrest was not there, and while the Godwin farm was being surrounded, the first shots were fired by the Union men, provoking a desperate fight. Lieutenant Cowan, leading the charge, contends, "In this attack, the Federals fired the first shot, the scar of which I bear to this day. Not a single man was killed after he surrendered, and any statements to this effect are wholly untrue." In either event, the incident did have the outcome of a massacre, as the Union suffers a loss of between twenty-five and thirty-five of its number killed or wounded, including the commanding officer, Lieutenant Royce, while the attacking Confederates claim but one casualty, the wounded George Cowan.[134]

Following the night attack, Forrest and his men continue on their journey, first to Plantersville and then across the Cahaba River to Marion, where they find the divisions of Jackson and Chalmers along with the soldiers who had managed to escape the debacle at Selma. They are, in the words of one of Forrest's cavalrymen, "whipped…war-worn soldiers." Nevertheless, "there was no weeping or wailing," remembers that same cavalryman. "Whipped or not…we felt assured that we had done our duty to our prostrate country…that we had fought it to a finish."[135]

Chapter 8

An Army of Occupation

On Monday morning, April 3, Wilson wakes up in the place he has chosen for his headquarters, the Gee House Hotel, where up until yesterday Richard Taylor had made his command center. "I was up and at work at an early hour," says Wilson. Indeed, he has much to do. His primary concern and the principal object of the entire expedition is to identify "the Confederate arsenal, gun shops, foundries, factories, and storehouses, and putting them under military guard." Once this is done, these facilities are, of course, "doomed to destruction." Wilson picks Edward Winslow, the brigadier commanding Upton's first brigade, to take charge of all the destruction. As an engineer from New England with considerable experience building railroads, the youthful Winslow is known to be resourceful enough to take on the huge responsibility of destroying Selma's vast military industry.[136]

Another prime concern of Wilson's is the reunification and resupplying of his army. He is uncertain as to the exact location of Edward McCook and the brigade that was sent to destroy the bridge at Centerville, but Wilson knows they're somewhere north of Selma with the supply train. What continues to trouble Wilson most, however, is the whereabouts of John Croxton's "Lost Brigade," still wandering somewhere around Tuscaloosa—as far as he knows, they may have been killed or captured. "We were," admits Wilson, "in the heart of the enemy's country, cut off from all communications." With no other choice, at daylight he sends Upton and his division to not only search for the missing brigades but also make sure that Forrest and Chalmers have retreated west of the Cahaba River. When Upton returns a few days later, he brings McCook, his brigade and the supply train, but no one has been able to learn anything about the mysterious disappearance of Croxton.[137]

Insofar as resupplying his army, Wilson has no problems. With the capture of Selma, he is able to seize all the supplies and goods he needs to replace those lost or consumed during his long march from North Alabama. Moreover, he commandeers a great number of horses and mules. So many, in fact, that there are plenty of replacement mounts for the cavalrymen whose animals have been worn out or injured in the campaign, as well as new mounts for those who had made the journey on foot. Yet even now, with his entire force adequately mounted, there are still one thousand mules and horses remaining. Afraid that the horses might fall into enemy hands after they leave, Wilson orders them "shot and thrown into the Alabama River." Mrs. C.E. Landis, remembering this incident, tells of the Yankees driving "every horse they could not take with them into a large vacant lot with a very high fence around it and shooting them till the blood ran through the gutters like water." Others are shot wherever they're found until they litter the city. "The carcasses were left lying in the roads, streets, and dooryards where they were shot," according to one historian. Although the Union soldiers do drag many of them into the river, hundreds are left for the citizens to deal with. Soon the air putrefies with the stench of rotting animals. Afterward, Wilson, apparently feeling a little remorse, writes, "The measure seemed cruel, but in war it is frequently necessary to do such things for self-protection as well as for the injury of the enemy."[138]

Throughout the early days of April, Wilson settles down to the business of occupying Selma and destroying every military target within it. During this time, he continues to worry about the safety of Croxton, and each day, he hopes to see him riding into Selma. He also uses this as an opportunity to inform Canby, who is now besieging Mobile, that on Sunday, April 2, he has taken Selma, a day he brags "was the greatest day in the history of the Cavalry Corps." But with the telegraph lines being in the enemy's hands, the mail now suspended and the trains no longer running, he must send the message by boat, down the Alabama River, a dangerous journey of 150 miles. "I found a middle-aged black man named Charles Marven, sensible, trustworthy, and well acquainted with the river," remembers Wilson. He then writes out the dispatch to Canby on tissue paper, and Marven conceals it in his clothing. Proud of the general's trust in him, Marven solemnly takes an oath to "deliver the message to Canby within five days unless killed on the way." And so he does.[139]

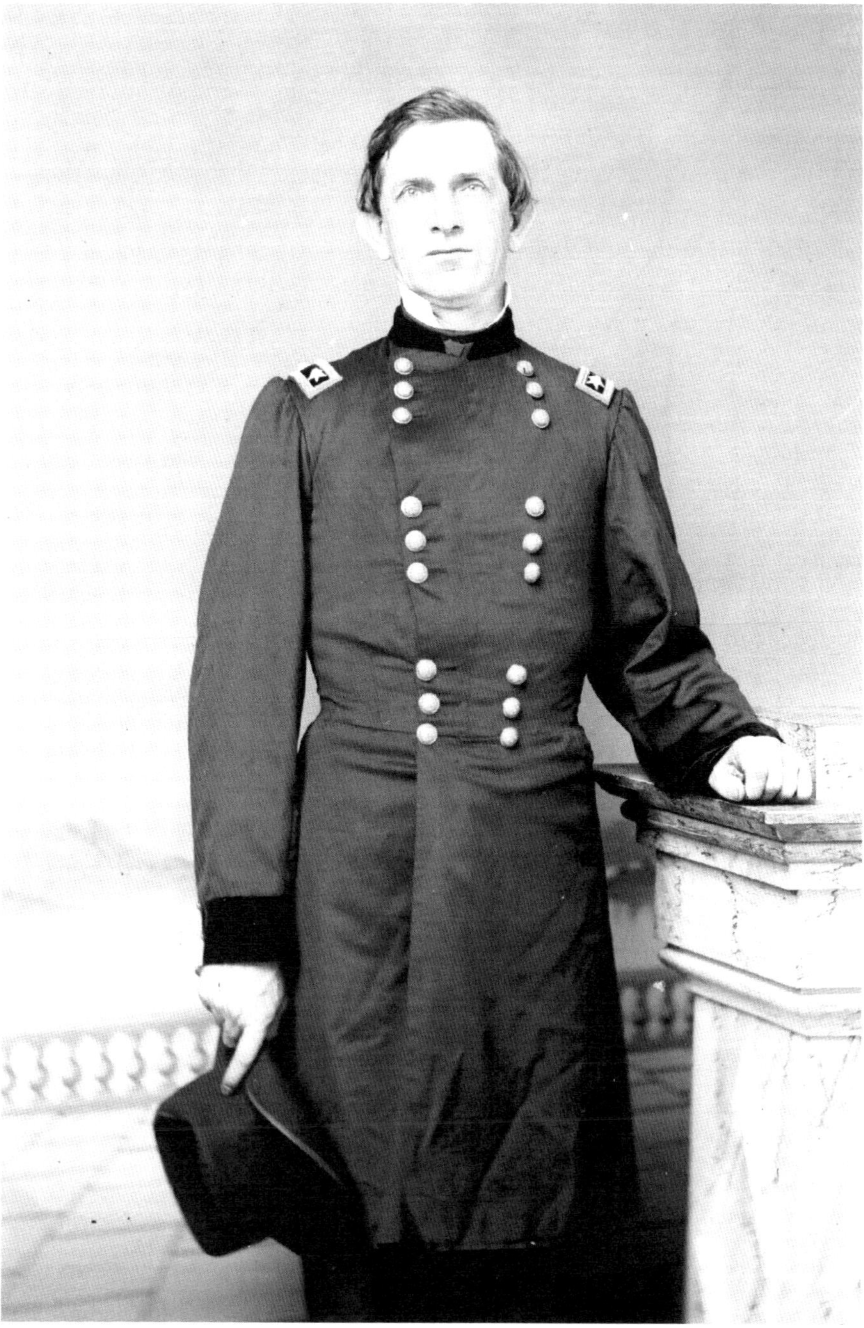

Union general E.R.S. Canby led the Federal forces in the campaign for Mobile. *Courtesy Library of Congress.*

Wilson's cavalry corps is, at least for now, an army of occupation. Although a great many of the private homes, such as Mrs. Landis's home, the home of Frank Siddons, now known as the Henderson House, and Marshall's Grove, Dr. Marshall's home, are seized by Federal officers and their staffs for living quarters or hospitals, most of the rank and file are camped on the plain just north of Selma. Here, the Union soldiers spend their time much like soldiers through the ages have done: washing clothes, cleaning their rifles, shoeing horses, writing letters, gambling with greasy cards and cursing the war. Some of them are assigned the duty of destroying Selma's military facilities, while others are given the task of working on the pontoon bridge that will carry them over the Alabama River once they depart the city. And, of course, there is always the unpleasant business of burying the dead and establishing hospitals for the wounded and sick. But many of the troops are idle, spending their time wandering the town's streets, looking at the devastation and talking with civilians. "The people are as badly used up as their town is," remarks Ohioan Isaac Jackson after chatting with them. They are, he believes, the "worst whipped people" there ever was.[140]

Following the horrific night of bedlam and destruction on Sunday, April 2, Union officers begin to restore some semblance of order. Thanks to Generals Wilson and Winslow, any citizen applying for protection for their family or property is readily granted it, and by Tuesday night, most of the homes have guards stationed on the premises. This, of course, is not to say that some soldiers are not still engaging in pillage, robbing and other indignities. They are. As with all armies, especially those that are occupying enemy territory, there is at least some measure of this. Sarah Ellen Phillips, along with her mother, endures one such incident when the "[Yankees] came galloping up to our very doors, ran up the steps and through the house…the very house seemed coming down on our heads. Mother's room quickly filled with ruffians, who seemed searching for hidden treasures, every bureau drawer and wardrobe shelf was soon run through or emptied on the floor…and began asking for money—for gold—running around here and there as if to find something." Afterward, for the remainder of "that perilous week," Sarah Phillips remembers "[e]very day we saw the smoke ascend and the heavens glow from the burning of some neighbor's ginhouse, corncribs or dwelling."[141]

But most of the smoke filling the skies above Selma comes from the burning of Confederate military facilities. "I cannot estimate in dollars the value of the public property here destroyed," admits Edward Winslow in his official report. Indeed, he has been a busy man. Between April 3 and April

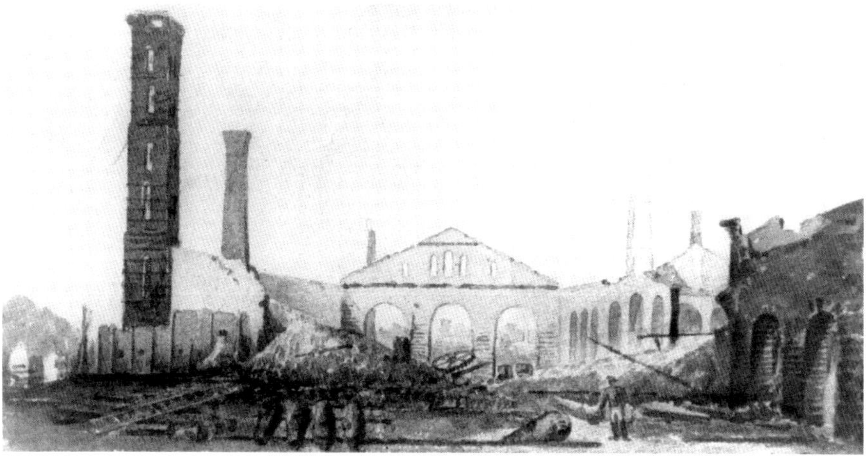

Ruins of Confederate Naval Foundry at Selma, Alabama, following Wilson's Raid. *Courtesy Alabama Department of Archives and History, Montgomery Alabama.*

9, Winslow and his men destroy "everything which could be of benefit to the enemy." This includes the Selma Arsenal, the largest of the facilities, consisting of twenty-four buildings holding siege guns, caissons, carriages, field pieces and more than one million rounds of small-arms and artillery ammunition; the Government Naval Foundry, with all the furnaces and machinery within its five buildings; the niter works, housed in eighteen buildings; the Selma Iron Works, occupying five buildings; the Powder Mill and Magazine, consisting of seven buildings; Pierce's Foundries, in two brick buildings with extensive machinery; two ironworks along with Phelan & McBride's Machine Shop; a horseshoe manufactory; the Selma Shovel Factory; numerous storehouses, filled with quartermaster's and commissary supplies; and roundhouses, locomotives, engines, machines and flatcars, all located on the tracks of the Alabama and Mississippi Railroad and Alabama and Tennessee Railroad, where they traverse Selma. This is by no means the extent of Winslow's destruction. The list goes on, but the results are the same, and Wilson sums it up best: "The blow was an overwhelming one to the Confederacy."[142]

During the occupation of Selma while Wilson waits for Winslow to complete the task of destroying the Rebels' war machine, Wilson continues to worry about the whereabouts and safety of John Croxton and his brigade. Since none of his own scouting parties has been able to find Croxton, it occurs to Wilson that the one man who might have information on him would be Forrest. After all, the Rebel commander would surely have knowledge of the location and strength of all the Union troops within his area of command. But Wilson knows he can't just come right out and raise the question with him. He's certain that Forrest would not knowingly provide his enemy with any useful intelligence. Besides, it would be an embarrassment for Harry Wilson, commander of a cavalry corps, to admit that he has lost an entire brigade of his men. There may, however, be a way to convince Forrest to innocently furnish some news on the whereabouts of Croxton. Since both sides have collected a number of prisoners during the campaign, he can request a meeting to ostensibly discuss a prisoner exchange—a ruse, much like the one back in February in Mississippi. In the course of their conversation, he might be able to coax the wily Rebel into providing some information about Croxton. At least it would be worth a try.[143]

So, on April 6, Wilson sends the young captain Lewis Hosea—the same clever officer who had met with Forrest before the campaign—to take a party across the Cahaba River and arrange a meeting between the two commanders. Hosea also takes a prisoner with him, a Rebel officer, as proof of his good faith. When his party reaches the bank of the river they are met by a group of civilians and rowed over to the small town of Cahaba. Before he can explain his mission to them the group—obviously concerned that their town is about to suffer the same fate as Selma—offers to surrender the town to the embarrassed Hosea. After hearing the reason for his trip and being assured that they have no cause for fear, he and his men are entertained at the home of one of the town's best families. For the young West Point graduate, he's delighted with their society, describing it as "the most delightful gratification of being with persons of education and culture." Later, this same day, Hosea returns to Selma, reporting to Wilson that he has made contact with one of Forrest's staff and arranged a meeting for the next day near the small town of Cahaba.[144]

Wilson, the "Boy General," is eager to meet the man who through the war years has become somewhat of a legend. Leaving Selma on the morning of April 7, Wilson and a few members of his staff ride to Cahaba, a distance of about ten miles, only to find the river swollen out of its banks and the bridges swept away. With no other choice, he would have to postpone the meeting until the river subsides, hopefully by the next day. "I reluctantly gave up the trip and returned to the city for the night," Wilson remembers. At ten o'clock the next morning, a Saturday, the general, Captain Hosea and another aide make the trip again, and this time they're able to cross the Cahaba and reach the home of a man named Matthews, a Union sympathizer, who has agreed to provide the venue for the meeting. After being introduced to Wilson, Matthews, who is known as Colonel Matthews, is astonished that the famous corps commander is so young. Even so, he receives them with true Southern hospitality. "He at once made me understand that I was a most welcome guest," says Wilson. After a brief conversation, Wilson forms a favorable opinion of his host: "I found a gentleman of great intelligence and high character and, although a slaveholder and rich planter, he had never given up his allegiance to the Union."[145]

Later, Forrest and his aides arrive at the Matthews home at one o'clock that afternoon. Glancing at the famous Rebel as he enters, Captain Hosea can't help but notice that he "was in common fatigue uniform, much soiled." And Wilson, seeing Forrest for the first time, seems a little disappointed in his physique. "I found him neither so tall nor so masterful in appearance as I expected." After the preliminary greetings and introductions, which are somewhat cool and reserved, the men are "summoned to a bountiful Southern dinner." After they're all seated the conversation turns more cordial, and the setting becomes more relaxed. By the time they finish their meal, Wilson recalls, "We were treating each other like old acquaintances, if not old friends."[146]

After dinner, the aides leave Forrest and Wilson alone, and the two men retire to the parlor for what turns out to be a "long but guarded conversation." Right away, Wilson senses Forrest's depression as he moves with cautious deliberation to the parlor with his left arm in a sling. Before they have even taken their seats, Forrest turns to Wilson with a steady gaze, saying, "Well, general, you have beaten me badly, and for the first time I am compelled to make such an acknowledgement."

Wilson, of course, realizes that this was the first battle Forrest has lost as a commander and attempts to mitigate the great general's morose spirits. "Our victory was not without costs," replies Wilson. "You put up a stout fight, but we were too many and too fast for you." Forrest nods in agreement yet knows he should give his adversary the credit he deserves.

"Yes, I did my best," concedes Forrest, "but, if I now had your entire force in hand, it would not compensate us for the deadly blow you have inflicted on our cause by the capture and destruction of our great arsenal, foundries, workshops, and storehouses at Selma."[147]

The conversation then turns to the battle just fought at Selma. They share their views about the details and strategies surrounding the fight. Forrest doesn't hesitate to admit to Wilson that his movements were too rapid for him to defend against and then confesses that in spite of pressing "every townsman from the oldest down to the schoolboys into the works," they could not repel the attack.

Although Forrest speaks freely about everything concerning Selma or past events, he is unwillingly to discuss anything relating to the future course of the war. Thus, when Wilson tries to steer the dialogue in that direction, he becomes very tightlipped. Wilson then launches into discussing a prisoner exchange, which is allegedly the purpose of the meeting in the first place. Again, just as he had done with his earlier meeting with Parkhurst and Hosea back in February, Forrest demurs, claiming a lack of authority.[148]

But Forrest does volunteer to give Wilson a count of the Federal prisoners he's holding. During the calculations, he inadvertently mentions Croxton and notes he had captured a few of his men. At the reference to Croxton, Wilson cocks his ears and becomes acutely attentive. Forrest then goes on to add that Croxton has been in and around Tuscaloosa, Trion and Meridian, "going practically where he pleased." Wilson, feigning indifference, is inwardly delighted. This is precisely what he had wanted to know, as it was the whole point of making this trip. "I brought the conference to a close," remembers Wilson, "with the excuse that it was getting late and I must return to Selma."[149]

Rising to leave, Wilson turns to Forrest and remarks in a solicitous tone, "General, I notice you are carrying your arm in a sling. I hope you are not badly hurt." Forrest shrugs it off, replying, "Oh no, merely somewhat severely bruised." Then, by way of explanation, he offers his version of a tale Wilson has undoubtedly already heard: "A young captain of yours singled me out at Ebenezer Church and rained such a shower of saber strokes on my head and shoulders that I thought he would kill me. While warding them off with my arm I feared he would give me the point of his saber instead of its edge, and, had he known enough to do that, I should not have been here to tell you about it."

Wilson, wanting to dismiss the incident as a bygone but also wishing to admonish the general about the future, cautions him, "Be more careful hereafter." Wilson goes on to warn him that many of his men would recognize him by sight and "would naturally regard it as a great feat of arms to kill him in battle." Without a hint of concern or emotion, Old Bedford, in a parting remark, prophetically says, "I am much obliged to you general, but I have no fear. I have faced death on a hundred fields and I am sure the bullet has not been cast which is to kill me." This, of course, is Wilson's first meeting with Forrest but hardly the last, as the two men will come to know each well after the war. And Wilson's impressions of his adversary now and in the future are established as someone endowed with "great firmness, excellent judgment, and inflexible will."[150]

Captain Hosea, however, comes away from the meeting with an unfavorable opinion of the Rebel general, a complete reversal of the one he had expressed back in February after his first interview with him. This time he sees him as "wounded, defeated, savage and unkempt…all the brutal instincts of the slave driver stood out unconcealed." Hosea's reassessed opinion of Forrest was, in all probability, formed a few days earlier as a result of the incident at the Godwin house the night of the battle at Selma. Hosea, like others, has heard all the stories and accepts them as fact that Forrest and his men had surprised Union lieutenant Royce and his cavalry detachment and killed them in a "cold-blooded and dastardly" manner.[151]

But Wilson has other things besides Forrest on his mind as he gallops back to Selma in the evening hours of April 8. Secure in the knowledge that Croxton is safe, he can now make ready for his next target. He also knows that Mobile is bound to surrender any day, if it hasn't already. And Canby, he believes, will not need his assistance in seizing the port city. Thus, for Wilson, his most logical and advantageous move is to cross the Alabama River, march east to Montgomery and then continue on through Georgia. By tomorrow he should be ready to move. The destruction of Selma's military arsenal has been accomplished, and his men are putting the finishing touches on the 870-foot-long pontoon bridge that will carry them across the river.[152]

Chapter 9

Cradle of the Confederacy

On Palm Sunday, April 9, Wilson's cavalry corps begins leaving Selma, crossing the pontoon bridge spanning the Alabama River. To the north, many miles away, in a small village in Virginia Ulysses Grant is accepting Robert E. Lee's surrender of the Army of Northern Virginia. And to the south, the Confederate forces on the eastern shore of Mobile Bay are laying down their weapons, compelling the city to surrender to General Canby. Of course, neither of these events is known to Wilson, his horsemen or the citizens of Selma as they watch the long procession trot across the sagging bridge of boats.

The crossing, beginning on Sunday, continues through the night and is not completed until the next day. Because much of the exodus occurs at night, Wilson orders several buildings along the river to be set afire to illuminate the way for what turns out to be a perilous passage. Watching the columns passing in twos, a staff officer notes in his diary, "The intense lurid glow of the burning buildings on the bank lit up the river, and the long lines of cavalry seemed to be marching upon its surface." All night, a rising river and treacherous currents propel huge logs and drifting trees to crash into the bridge, causing the long span to break three times during the crossing. But repairs are made, and tired men in skiffs do their best to deflect and guide the floating obstacles away from the bridge. Sometime during the night, General Andrew Alexander, who is supervising the men in boats trying to ward off the dangerous logs, experiences a horrifying moment. The strong current slams his boat into an anchor line, overturning it and spilling the general and his crew into the dark waters of the river. Fortunately, they are rescued by another skiff, but somewhere during the wild turmoil, Alexander is trapped between a big log and a pontoon, breaking three of his ribs and nearly crushing him to death.[153]

Reaching the south bank of the great river, Generals Wilson and Upton spur their horses up to the brow of a small hill where an Iowa cavalryman sees them "looking back to where disaster hung like a pall above the stricken city." Behind them, the sight is unforgettable as one Missouri horseman remembers, "In front was the dark river, with the bridge crowded. To our right were the burning buildings. To the left were the woods & in the rear were the remains of the arsenal....Here were a crowd of negroes of both sexes, of all colors & of all ages, there a squad of Confederate prisoners with their guards...& everything illuminated by the burning buildings." The sight moves one Union officer to contritely remark, "What a wreck of a place we have left."[154]

The next morning, April 10, as the last of the huge procession steps off the pontoon bridge, Wilson orders it dismantled. His corps has just begun moving eastward when he realizes what a multitude of souls he's now leading. Not only does he have his usual entourage of horsemen, wagon trains, pack animals and artillery, but now there are also ambulance wagons carrying the wounded who are well enough to travel and long lines of Rebel prisoners marching under guard. But what irritates Wilson and troubles him most are the throngs of civilians trailing his columns. "Crowds were following us," he grumbles, recollecting the nuisance of their company.[155]

Included in the mob of humanity trailing the raiders are some refugees who had fled from other war-torn places into Selma—some for safety and others for a chance at employment in the munition factories. In either case, the war has caught up with them again. They are now without jobs, homes or hope and, in desperation, are seeking some safe haven by drifting along in the shadow of the victorious army. But the vast majority of the traipsing horde are slaves who have escaped from the many plantations throughout the Black Belt and then fled to the Union army as their logical emancipators and protectors.[156]

For the frustrated Wilson, he decides that "vigorous measures" will be necessary to rid himself of so many extraneous followers impeding the progress of his march. He obviously cannot prevent the runaway slaves from "taking the road to freedom," but he can turn this "multitude to some useful purpose." Thus, on the first day of their journey, he begins organizing all the able-bodied black men into regiments where he will employ them as teamsters, train guards and road makers. As for the others—the older men, women and children—they will be "ruthlessly shut off." But even this harsh measure does not discourage them from straggling behind in the distance.[157]

Wilson is also not pleased with the idea of coping with so many Rebel prisoners. They are, of course, on foot, and even those who are healthy enough to make the march are exhausted from the long campaign. Prodding them along at the point of a bayonet is clearly hampering his corps' advance. But Wilson has a plan to solve this problem as well. Thinking back on it, Frank Montgomery, an officer taken prisoner at Selma, is clever in discerning the Boy General's method for ridding himself of the Rebel prisoners. "The prisoners, except the officers, were not closely guarded, and hundreds escaped, which, I think, was part of his plan to scatter them." For those not aggressive enough or inclined to escape, Wilson generously grants paroles along the way with the intention, he says, "[to] allow them to straggle back to Selma or to their homes as best they could." Such benevolence, however, is not extended to Montgomery and the rest of the officers. But before long, Wilson at least manages to have all of them mounted on animals confiscated from farms they pass along the road. "The officers," remembers Montgomery, "were mounted on all sorts of nags, mules, ponies and old plow-horses, with every variety of saddles and bridles." Not a dashing sight, but nevertheless, the column moves faster than before.[158]

The road to Montgomery takes Wilson and his raiders east fifty miles through the villages of Benton and Churchill and then to the town of Lowndesboro. With Forrest, Jackson and Chalmers all west of the Cahaba River, and apparently having no intention of following them, there is little opposition. There are, however, occasional skirmishes with small groups of Rebel cavalrymen from Abraham Buford's partial division coming out of Montgomery. Using natural defensive barriers along the route, such as a bridge spanning a creek or a swamp, they suddenly appear and open fire in a hit-and-run fashion and then quickly disappear into the dark woods. But just as Wilson claims, their main objective is in "keeping a careful watch on our movements."[159]

April 11 unfolds into another cloudy day, threatening to bring more rain, something the soldiers would clearly rather do without on this march. Because the Montgomery Road runs south of the Alabama River and generally parallel to it, much of the ground is low and marshy, often inundated with rising waters spilling over its banks. This routinely occurs, requiring the column to be delayed and the muddy road corduroyed before they can pass. After leaving the village of Benton, where they have camped during the night, the raiders cover only about a mile through a forest of longleaf pine. There the road abruptly sinks into a huge, mile-long swamp—the "Big Swamp," they call it. "Of all the swamps I ever experienced," a cavalryman in Upton's division says, "this is the swampiest." While waiting for the engineers and road workers to make the way passable, trooper E.N. Gilpin takes time to describe in his journal his view of the exotic swamp: "Majestic trees with hanging moss, tower above the gloomy waters, while a rank growth of juniper, nightshade and all manner of climbing and creeping shrubs and vines choke up the road and render it almost impenetrable."[160]

It takes most of the day for the long blue columns of horsemen, wagons and artillery to slog and drag their way through the dreary morass. As they finally emerge on the opposite side, they are, in the opinion of one soldier, "a muddy spectacle." But now the landscape suddenly changes into beautiful rolling country. Recalling the scene, Wilson opines, "We were at last within the richest planting district of the South and found it, not only untouched by war, but abounding in forage and provisions of every sort. The roads bordered by hedges of Cherokee roses, were redolent with spring perfumes. The march was, therefore not only rapid, but delightful and cheering." Indeed, for the troops, this country is beautiful, so different from the barren and inhospitable land they had traveled through in North Alabama only last month.[161]

Thirteen miles from Benton, the columns, which are strung out along the road for miles, begin passing through the town of Lowndesboro. Moving down the main street, the cavalrymen admire the great stately oaks, rose bushes and blossoming jasmine adorning the lawns and gardens of the antebellum homes of wealthy citizens. "This village," in the words of one officer, "is one of the most beautiful that we have yet passed through. It is built up of large, elegant mansions, and is inhabited by rich planters." "A dream world," an Iowa soldier calls it. And as if in a dream, the town is quiet, peacefully sleepy, with hardly any of its 1,500 people moving about. Wilson's medical director, Francis Salter, soon discovers the reason for the tranquility. "Smallpox was raging, and in some families had attacked all the members," he explains in his official report.[162]

By midnight, the last of the corps moves through the town of Lowndesboro and goes into camp five miles away, just eighteen miles from Montgomery.

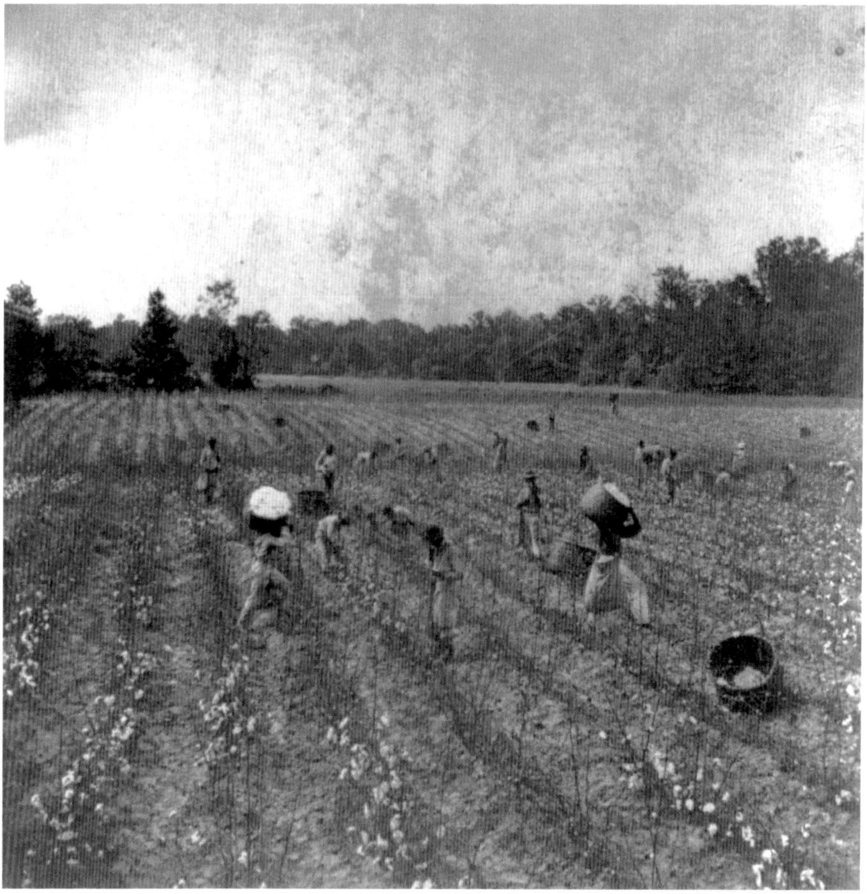

Slaves picking cotton on a plantation in the Black Belt near Montgomery, Alabama. *Courtesy Library of Congress.*

Sometime during the night, one of Wilson's officers brings him copies of the Montgomery newspapers, dated April 6 and 7. The papers contain news that Grant has forced Lee to evacuate Richmond, and Jefferson Davis has moved the Confederate government to Danville, Virginia. Although Wilson can't accept the Rebel papers as official information, they do serve to confirm the many rumors that they've been hearing for the past few days. At least satisfied that the Confederacy has "met with a great disaster in Virginia," Wilson makes the announcement to his corps. Just as he expected, their reaction is euphoric. "The whole army is cheering," a clerk on Upton's staff writes in his journal.[163]

To be sure, Wilson's raiders have good reason for cheerfulness when they break camp on the pleasant spring morning of April 12. Their mission, to this point, has been one of great success. News of Grant's victory in Virginia, and the hope that the end is near, has raised their spirits. They are now enjoying the rich bounty of the most fertile area of Alabama's Black Belt, yet untouched by war, and teeming with an abundance of good food for themselves and plenty of forage for the animals. But most importantly, they know that the leading elements of McCook's division under Colonel Oscar LaGrange are now only five miles from the city of Montgomery, the place many Southerners fondly refer to as the Cradle of the Confederacy.

Although the Confederates offered little resistance during Wilson's advance on Montgomery, and Forrest is nowhere nearby, the "Boy General" is almost certain that the city is fortified and will be "stoutly defended." After all, Montgomery is a manufacturing, commercial and distribution center served by three different railroads: the Alabama and Florida, the Montgomery and West Point and the Montgomery and Eufaula. Even though it does not produce nearly as much of the military equipment manufactured as Selma, it does boast a few arsenals turning out Enfield rifles and gunpowder. Also, vast amounts of cotton are moved through the city from surrounding plantations, down the Alabama River to the port of Mobile.[164]

But even more notable, Montgomery's importance is symbolic, epitomizing the spirit of the Confederacy. Alabama's capital is famously known as the first capital of the Confederate States of America. It was here, in February 1861, that Jefferson Davis left the Exchange Hotel on Commerce Street, made his way to the platform of the capitol portico and, after being sworn in as president, kissed the Bible and turned to ten thousand cheering people, saying, "So help me God." Adding to the drama, William Yancey, one of Alabama's most fanatical secessionists, stepped to the platform and with a shout cried, "The man and the hour have met." But now the hour has nearly arrived when the man and the government of his sworn allegiance will meet their ill-fated destiny.[165]

When Wilson's Raiders first entered Alabama, the citizens of Montgomery, like those in Selma and Tuscaloosa, paid little attention to the invasion. Much of their complacency and false hope can only be credited to Southern newspapers and their determination to keep the Confederacy alive through

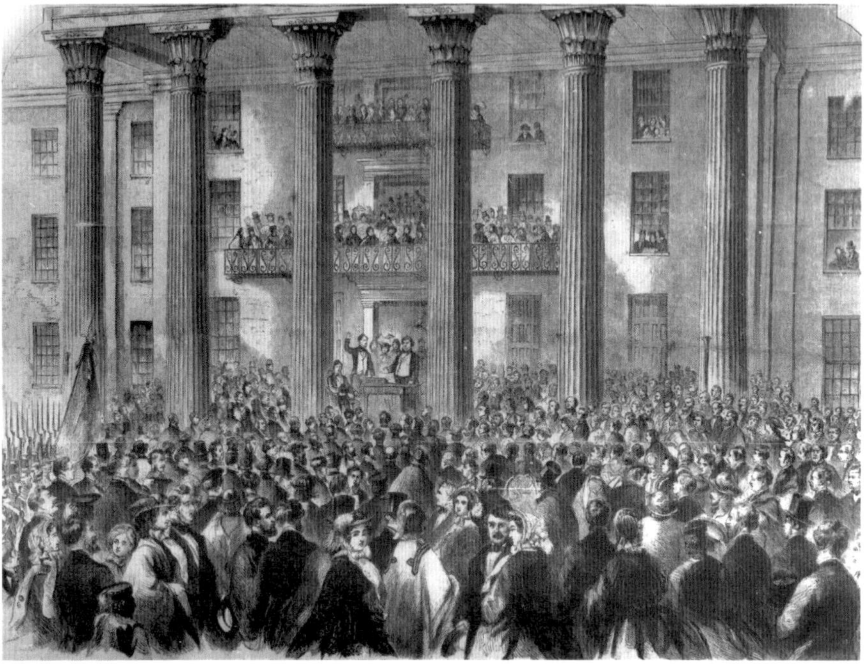

Inauguration of Confederate president Jefferson Davis in Montgomery, Alabama, 1861, from *Frank Leslie's Illustrated Newspaper. Courtesy Alabama Department of Archives and History.*

propaganda, often misleading readers on the progress of the war and the imminent danger of enemy attacks. At first, editors dismissed the threat of Wilson's presence with the assurance that he could never get past the dashing and brilliant Forrest. By the time Wilson reached Montevallo, the *Memphis Daily Appeal* claimed that the approaching Federal force was too small to be taken seriously. But the *Appeal*, having moved from city to city fleeing Yankee armies and now being published in Montgomery, has earned the sobriquet of the *"Moving" Appeal* and is hardly a paper to rely on for accurate reporting. The *Montgomery Daily Mail* convinces its readers that even if Forrest fails to stop Wilson's advance, the Union force will bypass Montgomery and move south to join Canby. Thus it's understandable, given the bravado and inaccurate information contained in these journals, that many civilians continue to be lulled into a false sense of security and are unprepared for intrusive Yankee visits.[166]

But all of the newspapers' exhortations begin to ring hollow on April 2, the day that Selma falls. They have been heard too often before and have proven false. Worse still, a few days after Selma is occupied, word of the Union soldiers' atrocities reaches the people of Montgomery, and a foreboding aura begins to take hold of the city. Because of its location in Central Alabama and outside of harm's way, Montgomery, like Selma, has had a large colony of refugees throughout the war, mainly women and children. Many of them are from the coastal cities of Mobile, Pensacola and New Orleans, and others are displaced from various regions around the South that have been turned into battlefields.

As early as 1863, Kate Cumming, a Mobilian, remembers visiting Montgomery and noted that the Exchange Hotel was "filled with refugees, fashionably dressed, and evidently making the best of their condition." Yet only a year later in 1864, the refugee population had swollen to the point that empty train boxcars were being used to house them. On Kate's next visit to the capital, she writes, "We were given possession of an empty car that had been set aside for refugees, which I named Refugee Hall." Now, with Wilson's Raiders in such proximity, these same refugees, along with many of the townspeople, are taking flight from Montgomery to the nearest safe haven. Among those making the exodus is the editor of the *Appeal*, moving once again, this time to Columbus, Georgia. However, it was later reported that he was captured in route by the Federal cavalry carrying "saddle bags filled with type, all that remained of the once prosperous Appeal."[167]

In early April, the city of Montgomery frantically begins preparing to defend itself. General Dan Adams, who has just finished fighting alongside Forrest at Ebenezer Church and Selma, has made his way to the capital after crossing the Alabama River and escaping the enemy cavalry. Nominally, at least, he is still in command of the District of Alabama and, according to the *Daily Mail*, promises the citizens "a full defense of the city." Joining in that blustering pledge is Alabama governor Thomas H. Watts, who proclaims, "The military authorities here are determined to defend the city. With my consent the seat of government shall not be surrendered as long as there is reasonable hope of defending it." At the same time, Watts requests the commanders in the neighboring counties to send their men to the defense of Montgomery. "Bring all the arms and ammunition you have or can get," he tells them. Then, appealing to their loyalty, he urges, "If you come we can save our state."[168]

But few come. The state capital does, however, acquire the services of General Abraham Buford and his cavalrymen. Buford, a seasoned veteran, is of course given command of the city's defense. Yet even with the combined commands of Dan Adams and Buford, they number, at most, about 1,500 men, considerably fewer than Forrest had the benefit of when Wilson overran

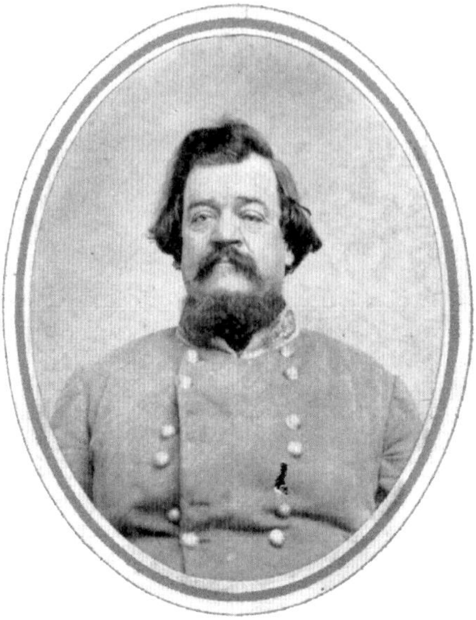

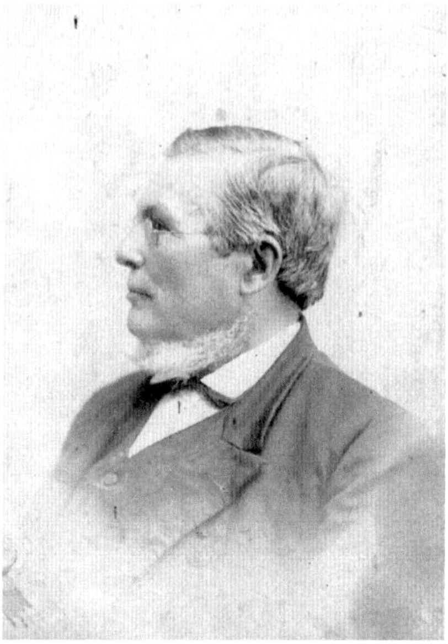

Left: Confederate general Abraham Buford. *Courtesy Alabama Department of Archives and History, Montgomery, Alabama.*

Right: Thomas H. Watts served as governor of Alabama from 1863 to 1865. *Courtesy Alabama Department of Archives and History, Montgomery, Alabama.*

Selma. So, with no other choice, Adams addresses the people: "Every man capable of bearing arms is called upon to volunteer for a limited period to aid in the defense of their capital and homes." Adams and Buford then do their best to prepare a defense. Volunteers and conscripts are drilled and supplied with arms and equipment. Slaves toil and sweat, piling up hundreds of cotton bales to barricade the streets. And cannons are rolled into the redoubts surrounding and fortifying the city.[169]

While Wilson draws closer with each passing day, more people leave the city. By the time the raiders reach the town of Benton on Monday, April 10, the streets are bustling with panicked citizens on their way out. They are, of course, not the only ones in flight. Duncan Graham, the state treasurer, is busy stuffing sacks with all the cash and other funds from the treasury's coffers. Graham then rides north to nearby Coosa County, where he and a relative, Daniel Crawford, spend the night burying the entire treasury of Alabama under the bank of a creek. Joining Graham in the exodus is Governor Thomas Watts and the rest of the bureaucrats in the state government, along with their families. However, they travel in a different direction: southeast, ninety miles away, to Eufaula in Barbour County, which also happens to be Governor Watt's hometown and is rumored to become the next capital of Alabama.[170]

Among those who stay behind is forty-year-old Sarah Follansbee, who finds herself in somewhat of a peculiar situation. Namely, she's a Massachusetts Yankee living in the Confederacy's cradle. Coming to Montgomery two years before the war to accept a position as a schoolteacher, Sarah has made close and lasting friendships with her neighbors. Yet as a staunch Unionist, she does not share the political beliefs of her Southern friends. But suddenly such ambivalent feelings do not seem so important. Like her neighbors, she finds herself caught up in the trepidations of war and a victim of the constant dread that accompanies it. As speculations of an attack increase, Sarah gathers her books, closes the school and writes in her journal, "Again the rumor the Yankees are coming!—Everybody under excitement. Military authorities had the cannon mounted at the fortifications—Cotton bales placed at the cross streets for barricades—At our corner 150 or more were placed—An artillery company with 8 pieces encamped opposite our house."[171]

Then, abruptly, all the efforts to ready the city's defenses come to a standstill. General Dan Adams has received word from Richard Taylor "to attempt no defense at Montgomery" but rather to move his infantry to Columbus, Georgia, and unite with Generals Howell Cobb and Abraham Buford for the defense of that city. Thus, on Tuesday morning, April 11, when the people of Montgomery begin to stir they discover that most of the troops have marched away during the night. Reactions to finding themselves defenseless vary. The *Montgomery Advertiser* contends that the news was received by the citizens with "stupor and no little dissatisfaction." But Sarah Follansbee disagrees, believing the city should be surrendered without a fight, and she claims that others share her opinion: "The citizens thought this foolhardiness [making a defense] with the small force he had." Dan Adams has apparently come to the same conclusion.[172]

Yet Adams seems unwilling to share with the city officials his plans for dealing with the arrival of the Union forces. Confused and worried about their fate, the city council appoints a committee to call on Adams and find out his intentions and proposals about protecting the city. The general, though, is vague in his response to their questions, saying only that he intends "to destroy the cotton in the city" before the Yankees can seize it. In this, he is "emphatic and inflexible," even though, as the committee points out, it would place the city in grave danger from the fires. Reporting on the meeting afterward, the town's newspapers claimed that Adams displayed an attitude that the public should not expect explanations from military men and told them as much: "Their query was based on the most idle curiosity, which he would not gratify. He did not know whether he would make a fight or not." Finally, he asks them why they had approached him in the first place. The committee then tells him that it is their intent to ride out and meet with the approaching enemy and arrange for the protection of the city. Indignant over such a proposal, Adams assures them he will arrest anyone who tries to leave the city.[173]

At five o'clock on Tuesday afternoon, Adams orders his remaining troops to set fire to the cotton, destroy all the whiskey and evacuate the city. Beginning with the cotton bales barricading the streets and then moving to each and every warehouse, containing an estimated ninety thousand bales, the troops apply the torch. Chaos ensues as more than $40 million of cotton is set ablaze. One witness recalls the scene: "Dense columns of smoke piled above the city and almost shut out the light of the sun. Women with affrighted countenances were seen running hither and thither, crying and wringing their hands, and hundreds of excited persons were endeavoring to secure the furniture from the adjacent houses." Believing that the raging inferno will consume the entire city, residents climb on their rooftops in a desperate attempt to prevent them from catching fire.[174]

Sarah Follansbee and the ladies from her neighborhood, fearing that their closely packed homes will be consumed, plead with the soldiers not to torch the cotton bales piled at the corner of their street. Soon a sympathetic Confederate officer appears, and seeing that the wind would clearly carry the fire onto the nearby homes, he "orders the men off." Grateful but still in fear that other soldiers might come "for the same purpose," Sarah, along with her friends and neighbors, defiantly keep vigil, seating themselves "on the bales till long after midnight."[175]

The citizens of Montgomery pass the night "in dreadful suspense." The city is in great danger of being consumed by the many fires and probably would have been except for what the *Montgomery Daily Mail* describes as a "miracle." During the night, the wind changes direction, "setting in from the east" and carrying the flames away from the city. This, together with the "great energy and courage" of the black fire companies, namely Alabama Fire Engine Company No. Two, saves the city from destruction. But what about the Yankees? That is an equally dreadful thought for the people on this night of terror. At any moment, Wilson's Raiders may appear. And when they arrive, what will they do? Loot? Murder? Rape?[176]

Fortunately, Mayor Walter Coleman and a committee of prominent citizens, mainly doctors and lawyers, have decided to ride out and intercept the Federals before they arrive and then to formally surrender the city "into the protection of the United States." This, of course, is what Adams prohibited them from doing, but Adams, Buford and the rest of the Confederate troops have left. And this group of men feel that submitting by surrender just might save Montgomery from the devastation and atrocities that Selma recently experienced. So, the party leaves Montgomery at 3:00 a.m. on April 12. Riding under a white flag, they find the Union lines near Catoma Creek. General Edward McCook, whose division is in the vanguard, is summoned to receive the surrender. After speaking with the mayor, McCook promises they will "protect all private property"—except, of course, property in use for military purposes. The committee then returns to Montgomery, satisfied that the town will not be burned or vandalized. Soon, Wilson and the rest of the officers and troops are notified of the surrender and "that there would be no fight." Everyone is surprised, and Wilson later admits, "They had not thought it possible that Montgomery, after having given such proud defiance at the outbreak of the Rebellion…would surrender without even a show of resistance."[177]

On the morning of April 12, shortly before eight o'clock, McCook leads his division into Montgomery. Trotting their horses up Market Street, passing a number of curiously anxious civilians, they continue to the capitol, where the U.S. flag is promptly hoisted over the statehouse. As the parade continues, regiment after regiment pass beneath the flag—or, as Wilson calls it, "the emblem of national authority." Here at the capitol, Mayor Coleman and the city council formally surrender the city to General McCook.

Having spent most of the night trying to protect their home from burning, Sarah Follansbee and her sister, Charlotte, are still asleep when their servant, Milly, rushes into the bedroom, shrieking, "Come, come see the Yankees." Racing outside to the fence, the sisters join Milly as they all gaze on "host upon host of blue coats." Indeed, the sight is impressive—as Sarah puts it, "A grand sight—the cavalry first—fine looking men—handsomely dressed—gleaming linen—as if right fresh from the laundry—brass buttons, brilliant epaulets also, sabers drawn & clashing, they made their entrance at full gallop."[178]

Many of the war-weary citizens, described by the *Advertiser* as "Union men of the 11th hour," cheer the blue columns parading the streets. Still others remain sullen, silently staring from their windows. But there are no incidents of violence, and McCook addresses the citizens gathered at the capitol, very

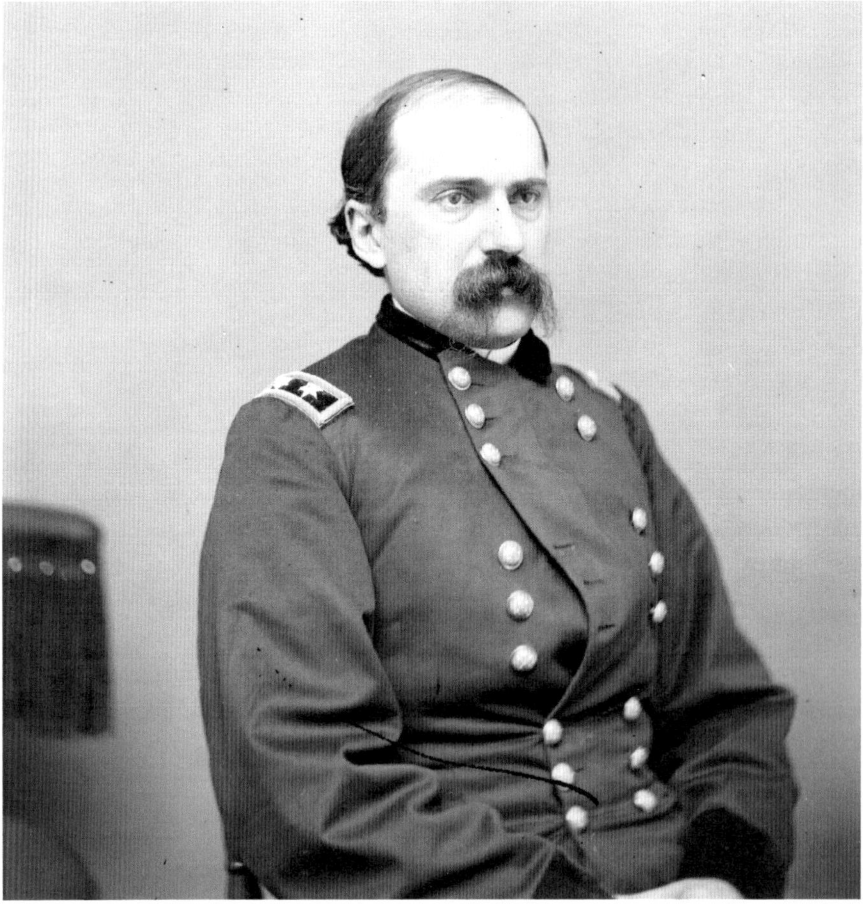

Union division commander General Edward McCook. *Courtesy Library of Congress.*

close to the spot where Jefferson Davis had made his inaugural address four years earlier, assuring them of protection. Montgomery will be spared. This same morning, Wilson repeats his orders to the rank and file of the corps that looting, marauding and vandalism will not be tolerated, emphasizing that anyone violating the code of "Christian soldiery" will be severely punished. With the war coming to an end, he wants no more incidents of destruction and pillage brought against a surrendered city. And except for a few isolated cases involving a few drunken soldiers on the outskirts of town, there are none. Clearly, his determined stance against laying waste to the city results in much better-behaved soldiers, as well as results in hospitable relations established with the citizens. Even the James Powell family, whose home at the corner of Moulton and Church Streets Wilson commandeers for his headquarters, are amiable and, in Wilson's words, "polite even to unwelcome guests."[179]

Wilson, though, is soon anxious to leave Montgomery and move to the northeast through Tuskegee and Opelika. This will complete his mission in Alabama, allowing him to cross the Chattahoochee River and ride into Georgia, where he will destroy the Rebel military machinery and railroads in Columbus, West Point, Macon and any other target standing in the path of his raiders. After all, Wilson is ever-mindful of his "duty to continue breaking things" until the war is officially ended. Thus, his stay in Montgomery is brief. Within two days of occupation, he completes the destruction of everything of value to the Confederate war effort. Although the city only contains a fraction of the property destroyed in Selma, it does include thousands of small arms, a foundry, shops, niter works, locomotives (along with their cars, railroad depots, tracks and trestles) and, finally, three steamboats that are burned for transporting army rations.[180]

Before leaving Montgomery, Wilson takes time to write his superior, George Thomas, briefing him on his progress and his plans. The telegraph is vintage Wilson, beaming of his confidence and spunk, and states in part, "There is no force to resist me, and I see no reasonable ground for fearing failure. My command is in magnificent condition; every man splendidly mounted, plenty of forage and supplies of all kinds....Campaign here is terminated, and everything ought to be pressed toward the Atlantic slope." The next day, April 14, having proclaimed this bravado to Thomas, Wilson mounts his horse and leads his raiders out of Montgomery.[181]

Chapter 10

"By Jingo, I'll Do It"

Before Wilson can begin his journey through Georgia, he must first lead his raiders through Tuskegee and Opelika. The road to Tuskegee continues east on to Columbus, where several bridges span the Chattahoochee River, the natural boundary between Alabama and Georgia. The road to Opelika generally follows the Montgomery and West Point Railroad in a northeastwardly direction to a few other bridges crossing the river thirty-five miles north of those at Columbus. For Wilson, it is imperative that his troops seize at least one of the better bridges before the Confederates can destroy them. He has no desire to be delayed building another pontoon bridge over the Chattahoochee, which is still out of its banks from the spring rains. Thus, Wilson decides to divide his force just east of Tuskegee, sending the rangy New Yorker Oscar LaGrange and his brigade through Auburn and Opelika to West Point while he continues on the road out of Tuskegee, leading the main force to the twin cities of Girard, Alabama, and Columbus, Georgia.[182]

As the raiders begin their forty-mile journey from Montgomery to Tuskegee, Oscar LaGrange's brigade of McCook's division again takes the lead. After traveling only three miles, they begin encountering Rebel cavalrymen firing on them from behind rail barricades in the road. At each roadblock, raiders from the First Wisconsin Regiment at the front of the column charge, chasing them to their next prepared obstruction, then charging them again and so on. This running fight continues, according to LaGrange, for thirty-eight miles. At times, the pursuit of the Rebels is so rapid that they're caught before they can make their way to the next barricade. So it's hardly surprising that along the way to Tuskegee, one hundred Confederate prisoners are taken, while only twelve are killed. LaGrange's losses are light, with one killed and seven wounded.[183]

LaGrange and the leading elements of Wilson's Raiders make camp on the night of the fourteenth about one mile from Tuskegee. This sends the town into a fit of excitement, as the citizens worry about the Yankees' arrival and what it will mean for them. Although they know there will be no defense offered and a fight will not take place, they are apprehensive about their buildings and homes being destroyed. But when LaGrange and his brigade enter the town early on the morning of April 15, they continue passing through, remaining only long enough to accept the mayor's surrender and then leave the main road on their way to West Point.[184]

Somewhere around noon, Wilson and the rest of the corps begin parading through the town that the "Boy General" describes as a "beautiful one"—"the seat of education and refinement for an extensive region." His comment, of course, is in reference to the many private schools and seminaries located here. Once again, the mayor surrenders the city and begs "protection for person and property." And once again, he's reassured by the Yankee general that his request will be granted.[185]

But for Carrie Hunter, "[a] dread hour has arrived." She is a young art student enrolled at the Methodist-sponsored Tuskegee Female College, which will one day become Huntington College. Having lost both her brothers, killed in battle only last year, Carrie is convinced that "the murderers of our martyred brothers" will destroy the town and the college. News has since reached the people of Tuskegee that the Yankees burned the university in Tuscaloosa and that they should expect the same fate for their own schools. Carrie agrees, confessing to her diary, "What will become of us the Lord only knows."[186]

Although she's apprehensive over her future providence, Carrie will soon learn that for the most part, her fears are unnecessary. By this time, with so many rumors and newspaper accounts that Lee has surrendered or is about to, along with an official confirmation received this very day that Richmond had indeed fallen, Wilson has no intention of bringing about the destruction of a surrendered city. In fact, with the demise of the Confederacy all but complete, he is now doing his best "to impress the people with the good behavior and discipline of the Northern cavalrymen." After posting guards on all the street corners and taking the "usual precautions" against marauding and mischief by his soldiers, Wilson makes his headquarters "at the best hotel." However, he only remains there for five hours, and during this short stay, he recalls that "the mayor, the leading citizens, and the principals of the seminaries called to pay their respects." To the general's surprise, nearly all of the callers are complimentary of the conduct of his army. In fact, for Wilson, their appreciation is so exaggerated that "the situation was becoming embarrassing…and I was anxious to put an end to it."[187]

The sole exception of a townsperson who is not complimentary comes in the person of a "dignified and serious woman," who just happens to be the editor of the *Tuskegee Press*. She tells him of a detachment of his soldiers who are threatening to destroy her printing press because it prints a "rebel newspaper." Then she politely asks "if this was in accordance with my orders." After Wilson replies that this is "our policy and practice to break up all the rebel newspapers we could find," she loses her temper. Ranting furiously, she declares that she should have "expected nothing better," and she "never believed that Yankees could be as liberal or enlightened as they pretended to be." Continuing the tirade, she tells Wilson that they are surely "enemies of religion and education" since her press is the only means of "printing Bibles and schoolbooks." "But Madam," Wilson interrupts as the lady editor pauses to catch her breath, "You said nothing at first about printing Bibles and schoolbooks, and you frankly admit that you have been publishing a rebel newspaper." So, after getting her assurance in writing that she will print nothing "inimical to the Union or the Constitution, but will confine her press exclusively to the publication of Bibles and schoolbooks," Wilson orders her printing press spared from destruction.[188]

Although Wilson's stay in Tuskegee is brief and the town is spared from destruction, some looting apparently does take place. After the raiders ride out of the city in a "violent rainstorm" on Saturday afternoon, April 15, word spreads through town that at least some of the bluecoats had not been on their best behavior. "Well! The Yanks have come and gone," Carrie Hunter announces in her diary, "and left us safe and sound with our house standing over our heads—a piece of clemency quite extraordinary." But then she hatefully adds, "Nearly all our friends lost their jewels and valuables." In one final jab, she describes their nefarious doings and bad manners with the uniquely Southern and imaginative expression: "Yankeefied Yankeeism."[189]

In a "pelting rain," Wilson and his staff follow the rear guard out of Tuskegee and plod along the muddy road about six miles before reaching a "rich and favorably located" plantation. Here they spend a comfortable night, and at dawn the next morning, they continue the march to Columbus, Georgia. Meanwhile, Oscar LaGrange's brigade, which was detached from the main force at Tuskegee on April 15, travels twenty-seven miles on the road to Opelika and West Point and then goes into camp at Auburn, Alabama. They are under orders from Wilson to "burn the trestles and stations" along the Montgomery and West Point Railroad and to "capture the fort and garrison covering the bridge across the Chattahoochee." Although the town of West Point isn't a manufacturing center, it is an important rail center. Here terminate the Montgomery and Atlanta lines, each with different gauges. Trains stop and cargo must be transferred from one to the other. Hence, there is a huge railroad yard full of locomotives and cars, a target Wilson intends to destroy.[190]

The leading elements of LaGrange's brigade, consisting of two Indiana regiments and a battery, leave Auburn well before sunrise on April 16, galloping north and following the railroad. At 10:00 a.m., the horsemen rein in their mounts as they come within range of an earthen fort sitting on a rise on the Alabama side of the Chattahoochee and protecting the railroad bridge crossing the river. The two Hoosier regiments, armed with their Spencer carbines, take cover within shooting distance of the fort and begin a sporadic fire. At the same time, the artillery battery unlimbers its guns and begins lobbing shells in "a steady, well-directed fire." The firing continues until early afternoon, about 1:30 p.m., when LaGrange arrives with the rest of the brigade.[191]

Through the smoke from the guns, Oscar LaGrange nudges his horse forward, studying the Rebel fort, which he describes as "a remarkably strong earthwork, thirty-five yards square, surrounded by a ditch twelve feet wide and ten deep, situated on a commanding eminence and protected by an abatis." He also sees that the structure is armed with three cannons: a thirty-two-pound siege gun and two twelve-pound Napoleons. LaGrange estimates that the structure is defended by "265 desperate men" and known as Fort Tyler, presumably named after the man who is commanding the Rebel garrison, Robert Charles Tyler.[192]

The thirty-two-year-old Tyler, distinctive by his chiseled jaw and waxed moustache, is another rare case of a soldier enlisting as a private and rising to the rank of brigadier general. His rapid promotions were due in part to the fact that he has fought bravely in nearly every engagement in the western theater. He bears wounds from at least three battles, the last of which he received at Missionary Ridge, so serious that one of his legs had to be amputated. After this last maiming, the war-torn Tyler doesn't rejoin the Army of Tennessee but assumes a post at West Point, Georgia, which up until this point in the war has enjoyed a peaceful existence.[193]

But now the crippled general is faced with making what one of his soldiers calls "a hopeless defense." As LaGrange approaches the little town of West Point, Tyler hurries to assemble all the men he can find to defend the fort and guard the bridges. His best efforts, however, only result in a motley conglomerate of men: furloughed troops en route to rejoin the army, soldiers convalescing from wounds, militiamen, hospital workers and civilians. Of this group, only about one hundred are actually soldiers, according to Tennessee veteran W.J. Slatter, who proudly boasts, "I was in the fight from start to finish."[194]

The Union attack gets underway at three o'clock in the afternoon. LaGrange takes one of the Hoosier regiments, the Fourth Indiana, and swoops through town, scattering some Rebel cavalry and capturing both bridges, which was their primary goal all along. The charge is unexpected and surprises the Rebel defenders in the fort, as well as the few in town guarding the bridges. So sudden is the attack that they had no time to set fire to them before the Yankee horsemen were on top of them. But those in the fort manage to fire at the charging horsemen with their thirty-two pounder, loaded with grapeshot. However, the shot falls short, doing little damage, except killing the horse Colonel LaGrange is riding. While the fort's defenders are distracted by the cavalry charge, the rest of LaGrange's brigade dismounts and rushes the bastion from three sides. The Union artillery battery covers their advance "with a most accurate fire"—so accurate, in fact, that one of the battery's guns, firing from a distance of six hundred yards, manages to strike "the 32-pounder planted in the fort," putting it out of action. For a moment, it appears that the dismounted cavalrymen will succeed in taking the fort. But then the troops realize it's impossible to get across the huge ditch surrounding the fort with the Rebel riflemen pouring fire down on them from behind the earthen walls of the fort.[195]

While most of the cavalrymen are now pinned down and held at bay, others are ripping the boards from nearby houses and barns for the long planks that will serve as a bridge to cross the ditch. Quickly, another charge is ordered. This time the bluecoats throw their planks across the ditch and manage to cross but are driven back again as they try to scale the walls. LaGrange, now determined to take the fort, orders a concentrated artillery fire from his battery. When the smoke clears, all the Rebel cannons have been silenced, and the troops move forward again. The Rebels, now nearly out of ammunition, begin hurling lighted shells over the wall. Finally, in desperation, they start throwing stones along with their empty rifles down on them. But in the end, the bluecoats break into the fort and find forty-six Confederates dead or wounded, most having been shot in the head while firing over the wall. Union losses, on the other hand, only number thirty-six in what Wilson describes as a "remarkable performance." Among the Confederate dead is General Robert Tyler, his sword still in his hand. His second in command, Colonel James Fannin, knowing that further resistance is hopeless, surrenders the garrison and the town. Recalling the event years later, one of the survivors, W.J. Slatter, who was taken prisoner, pays a high tribute to the little band of defenders: "Never were there more courageous men."[196]

This same day, thirty-five miles to the south, Wilson's main force has passed the town of Crawford and moves steadily toward Girard and Columbus, twin cities separated only by the Chattahoochee River. Taken together, the population is about twelve thousand, many of whom are refugees driven here from other places. For those who have been chased from one place to the next, the town represents one of the last havens of protection they have left. Like Selma, it's a river city and a factory city. Thus it has a naval yard, textile mills and factories, all manufacturing a variety of products and materials for the Confederate war effort. Furthermore, just as Wilson claims, Columbus is "the door to Georgia." So it's understandable that the "Boy General" has identified the city as one of his primary targets for destruction and equally understandable that the Confederacy is determined to protect its last major manufacturing center.[197]

"The city of Columbus will be defended to the last," or so proclaims the *Columbus Sun* on the very day Wilson's Raiders are approaching the gates of the city. The problem—always the problem—is that there are simply not enough men left to offer any serious defense. Between two and three thousand men are available. But most are unfit for combat. Besides a few exhausted cavalrymen, they are mostly reserves, factory workers, local militia too old or too young for service and disabled veterans, some missing fingers, a limb or an eye or hobbled with a variety of other war wounds.

These are the men expected to stand "to the last" behind a line of defensive fortifications that are woefully inadequate and hold back a force as great as Wilson's Raiders. Responsibility for such a hopeless duty rests with a worn-out, fifty-year-old Georgian, General Howell Cobb. He's also the man with the unenviable task of commanding the entire District of Georgia, a state that has already felt the terrible wrath of Sherman and his army, and now must deal with another Yankee devil in the person of Wilson and his raiders. Even though Cobb, once a proud secessionist, has thrown "his whole heart and fortune into the Confederate cause," the double-chinned, portly general is in poor health as he strives to defend his state in these last days. Only four years earlier, he was a member of the committee that administered the oath of office to Jefferson Davis on the portico of the capitol in Montgomery. Now, knowing the end is near, he will stand guard on his native soil for the last time and make the "best fight" he can.[198]

The Confederate defenses protecting Columbus and the bridges spanning the Chattahoochee are located on the Alabama side of the river in and around the town of Girard, which in the future will be renamed Phenix City. Forts and rifle pits have been built here to protect the approaches to the three bridges, since the only way for Wilson to capture the factory city of Columbus is to fight his way over at least one of them. This, of course, is precisely what he intends to do on the afternoon of April 16.

Wilson taps Emory Upton to lead the attack and "have the post of honor at Columbus." Elated with his assignment, Upton hurries to position his two brigades, one under Edward Winslow and the other led by Andrew Alexander, to attack and seize the bridges into Columbus. Upton wastes no time in ordering Alexander and his lead regiment of Ohioans to charge the southernmost bridge. "Can you give us the bridge across the Chattahoochee?" Upton asks as he rides to the front of their column. Shouting back, the horsemen say they will try and then gallop off through the town of Girard, surprising and scattering the Rebels in their path. Firing their Spencer carbines, Alexander's bluecoats continue driving them down the road and across the bridge. And for a brief minute, Upton, watching the attack from a hill, becomes excited, thinking that his troops have surely taken the bridge. But before the Ohioans can cross, the gray defenders rally just long enough to put their torches to the turpentine-soaked bridge from the Georgia side, thus putting an end to "the pursuit, as well as the capture of Columbus from that direction."[199]

But Upton is undaunted. Putting the spurs to his horse, he races northward toward the other bridges. Meeting Wilson along the way, the two

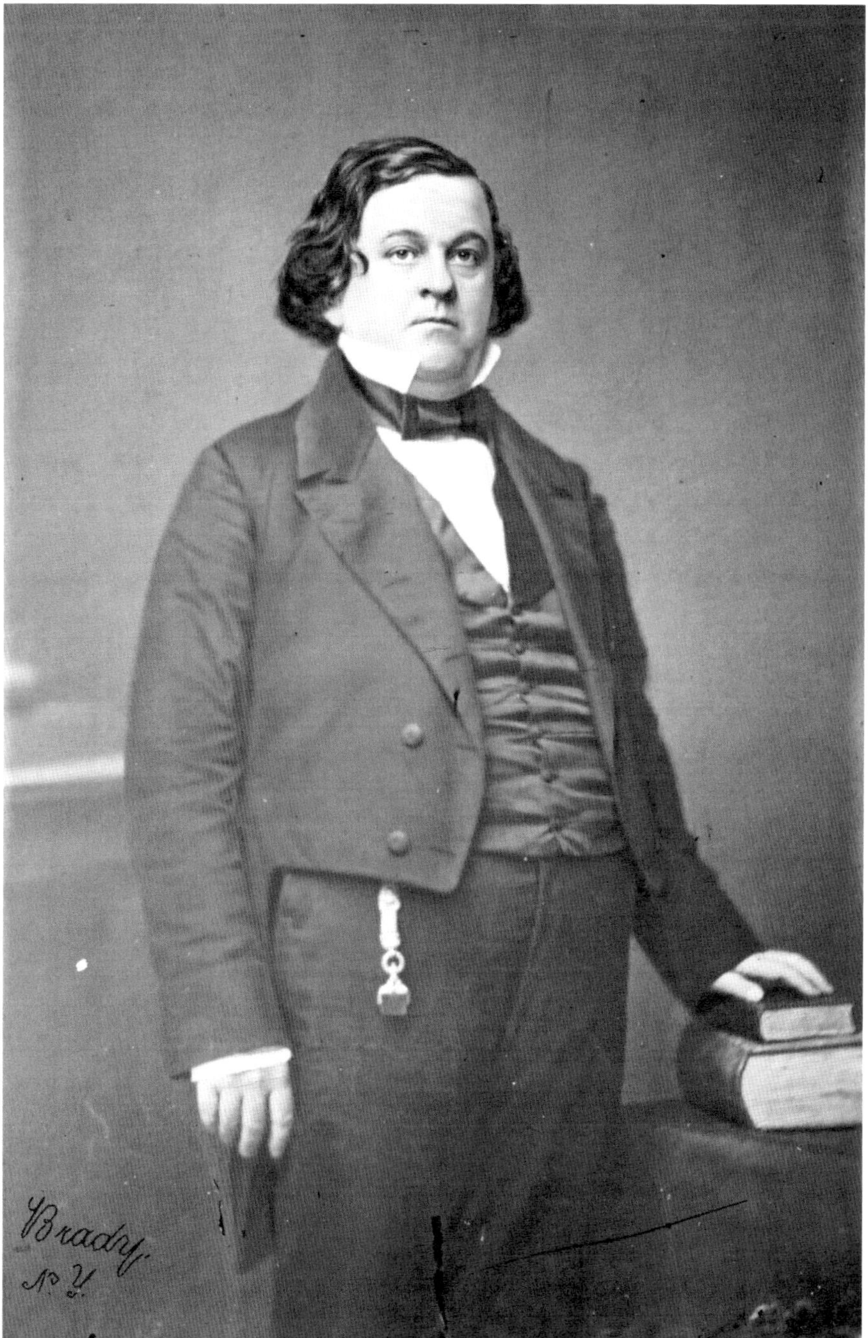

Confederate general Howell Cobb commanded Confederate forces in Georgia. *Courtesy Library of Congress.*

men reconnoiter the Confederates defending the footbridge and railroad bridge on the north side of town and decide that the main attack should be made here, with Edward Winslow's brigade striking the enemy first from the northwest. It's about four o'clock as Upton rides off to find Winslow and place his brigade into position for the attack. A half hour later, though, Upton returns to Wilson, "riding up rapidly and saluting with impatience."[200]

"Everything is ready for the assault," Upton pants breathlessly, "but I cannot find Winslow and must delay the attack till he is in position."[201]

Having passed Winslow's brigade earlier in a nearby wooded valley, Wilson points out their position to Upton. It's unclear what degree of embarrassment this may have caused Upton for losing one of his brigades, but the energetic New Yorker never mentions it. Instead, he expresses remorse at losing this opportunity. "But it is now too late," he tells Wilson apologetically. "It will be dark before I can get him into position and lead the division to the attack."[202]

After mulling over the situation facing them, Wilson reminds himself that by this time, his raiders have become "pretty well accustomed to night fighting and its advantages." A night attack might result in "less loss and greater success than one in full daylight." So, turning to Upton, the young general tells him, "You will make all your arrangements to attack at 8:30." Upton, surprised and now trembling with excitement, replies, "Do you mean it? It will be dark as midnight by that hour and that will be a night attack, indeed!" Nodding his consent, Wilson then instructs his division commander to get everything ready to attack. Turning to Wilson with "flashing eyes," Upton exclaims, "By jingo, I'll do it; and I'll sweep everything before me!"[203]

Upton, it seems, was correct in saying that by 8:30 p.m. it would be "dark as midnight." And so it is on this moonless Sunday night as Winslow's brigade waits for the order to attack. Six companies of the Third Iowa Cavalry, commanded by a colonel named John Noble, stand dismounted in the road only two hundred yards from the Rebel lines. Behind them, on horseback, in columns of four, is the Tenth Missouri Cavalry, led by young Lieutenant Colonel Frederick Benteen, who after the war will continue his army career, serving in the Seventh Cavalry under the colorful George Custer and who will have the hapless distinction of being remembered as the officer who failed to promptly come to Custer's rescue at the Battle of the Little Bighorn. Following Benteen's horsemen and also mounted are the cavalrymen of the Fourth Iowa, commanded by Lieutenant Colonel John Peters. Together the brigade numbers a little over two thousand men.[204]

One of the men waiting in formation is Captain Hinricks, an officer in Benteen's Missouri Regiment, who gives a vivid description of the ordeal by fire on this night: "It was dark as pitch, not a sound could be heard anywhere." Then, only moments before the order to attack is given, the Confederate muskets and artillery open up, as if they had somehow sensed what was coming. "All of a sudden there was a shot, another, and in a second 10,000 more," remembers Hinricks. "The whole country seemed to be alive with demons." When the order is given to charge, the Missourians lunge forward on horseback, hooves clopping, following John Noble's dismounted Iowans, who have already raced through the Rebel outer lines. As the balls hiss and sing around them and shells scream overhead, bursting into blinding "blue lights," Hinricks is awestruck. "This was the first time that I ever saw shelling during night time," he later recalls. "It is a beautiful but awful spectacle."[205]

Seeing the Rebels falling back in confusion from the outer lines to the inner entrenchments and the bridge, Wilson spurs his horse through the dark, which is lit only by "starlight and the enemy's guns." Looking for someone to take advantage of the early break in the enemy lines, he finds Benteen and his Missourians. "I personally ordered Benteen with the Tenth Missouri, to enter the captured works and follow the road through the inner entrenchments to the bridge." This they do, but only two companies succeed in fighting their way through the entrenchments to the bridge. Although they succeed in capturing the bridge, their possession of it is only temporary. A reinforcement of Confederates discovers their presence and launches a furious counterattack, pouring a heavy fire into the Missourians from all directions and managing to retake the important span and reestablish their lines. At this point, Emory Upton takes personal charge of his brigade. Gathering both Iowa regiments and the Missourians, he shouts in a high, shrill voice, clearly heard over the rattle and roar of the conflict, "Charge em! Charge em!"—a din that Wilson describes as "hideous." Although the charge is disorderly, with Upton's men confused and bewildered in the dark, the defending Confederates are inexperienced, outgunned and outnumbered and are much worse off. Now with the added punch of the entire brigade, the bluecoats, yelling, cursing and firing, collapse the Rebel lines and charge over the bridge onto Georgia soil.[206]

Bedlam ensues as the Confederates retreat into Columbus. Among those in flight is William Martin, a farmer too old for service. Only this morning he had been at his home in Silver Run, a small Alabama village on the railroad, ten miles north of Girard. Hearing that the Yankees were quickly approaching from the west, he and eight of his neighbors volunteer to go along with the local home guard and join in the defense of the city.

After the Rebel line breaks, the bridge becomes crowded with soldiers, both blue and gray, some on foot and others on horseback, all frantically pushing and shoving their way across the narrow span to gain the Columbus side. "In the dark, friend and foe became mixed," remembers one Southerner. William Martin, joining in the chaotic retreat, stumbles and falls into a ditch just as he crosses the bridge. Losing his gun, he is taken prisoner by a Yankee soldier on horseback. As he's being prodded down the street by his captor, a Rebel colonel on horseback is galloping down the street, swinging his sword and calling on the troops to rally. Seeing the high-ranking officer, the Yankee guard spurs his horse toward him, knocking Martin down in the process and then shooting the Rebel colonel. Then the Yankee quickly dismounts and begins rifling through the pockets of the dead colonel, and Martin, now seeing his chance to escape, races off into the black night.[207]

By now, chaos has gripped the city. "A perfect panic," says a local doctor, who later describes the distressing scene to one of his nurses: "Women and children were running through the streets like people deranged, and men, with mules and wagons, driving in every direction." Even the soldiers, blue and gray, become confused in the pandemonium. "Everybody blundered around in the dark, fighting pretty much at random," remembers Fanny Andrews, a young Georgia girl. "If a man met someone he did not know, he asked whether he was a Yank or a Reb, and if the answer did not suit his views he fired." Finally, with defeat inevitable, every Southern soldier and civilian who is able to escape does so, including the Rebel general Howell Cobb, his staff and about 600 troops. Those who are left throw themselves on the mercy of the raiders, and 1,500 men are made prisoners. The number of Confederate killed and wounded is never reported, although one Union officer contends that the following day the Rebels were still picking up their dead and wounded. Wilson, however, claims only 24 of his men killed, citing that "darkness had protected the fighting men of both forces." And according to the raider's commander, by eleven o'clock on the night of the battle, "absolute quiet and order reigned throughout the city."[208]

Assuming "absolute quiet and order" did reign on Sunday night, it somehow vanishes on Monday morning, replaced by a nightmare of hellish destruction and mayhem. At first light, Wilson unleashes Edward Winslow and his men to destroy the manufacturing facilities in the twin cities, a process they have refined to a diabolical art during this campaign. Just as they had done in Selma, "everything within reach that could be made useful for the further continuance of the Rebellion" is destroyed: locomotives, freight cars, machine shops, the naval armory and shipyard, rolling mills, machinery, ironworks, foundries, mills and factories and seven warehouses containing 100,000 bales of cotton. Of course, the burning and devastation of the facilities will result in about five thousand people being unemployed, a fact not lost on those affected. As a consequence, these same people take the opportunity to pillage and plunder everything left after the destruction. Their greed, according to Winslow, is "seemingly insatiable," and he writes in his after-action report, "The citizens and Negroes formed one vast mob, which seized upon and carried off almost everything movable, whether useful or not."[209]

On the evening of April 17, as Wilson and his raiders ride out of Columbus, the city lays smoldering in rubble and ashes. With this last victory, the "door to Georgia," as Wilson calls it, has now been opened, and they will continue on to Macon. Although Wilson expects Macon to offer a fight, it never occurs, as Howell Cobb sees the futility of resisting and surrenders the city on the evening of April 20. Wilson, at last, will rest his troops in Macon and await a rendezvous with LaGrange and, hopefully, the long-lost Croxton.[210]

Chapter 11

Return of the Lost Brigade

Since April 8, when he met with Forrest in Cahaba, James Wilson has not been overly troubled over the well-being of John Croxton and his brigade. After all, Forrest has assured him that his brigadier was still around Tuscaloosa, "going practically where he pleased." Nevertheless, Wilson is still concerned over his long absence and says so in a letter to General Thomas on April 13 after taking Montgomery: "I am anxious… to have Croxton join me as soon as possible." Had Wilson known all the troubles and perils Croxton has been facing up to this point, he would certainly have reason to worry.[211]

After seizing and destroying the town of Tuscaloosa, Croxton's movements and plans have all been designed around the goal of rejoining Wilson and the main corps. The trouble is that he's unsure of their exact whereabouts. But this is only one of his many problems. He's deep in hostile territory with no lines of supply or communication. Rebel cavalry from Forrest's command are crawling all over the countryside and might show up anywhere he decides to move. His men have but few rations, and food and forage are scarce. The country is inhospitable with poor roads and many unfordable streams and rivers. On top of everything else, Yankees, this far south, are rarely welcomed, and the people they encounter along the way are anything but amiable.

On April 5, Croxton leads his 1,500 horsemen out of Tuscaloosa, riding southwest. This, he feels, is the safest direction to move since Red Jackson's brigade is still being reported in the area to the south and east. Besides, Wilson had instructed him earlier that "if practicable," his secondary mission should be to destroy the Alabama and Mississippi Railroad coming out of Meridian. And now, with his options for movement being limited, this is the work he will carry out. This same night, with his brigade camped twenty-five miles from Tuscaloosa, Croxton dispatches a company of horsemen from the Sixth Kentucky Regiment under Captain William Sutherland to leave the main column and ride toward Columbus, Mississippi, feigning an attack on that city. Along the way, Sutherland is instructed to scout the country and "collect all the information possible" and then turn to the south and rejoin the main column at one of the crossings on the Tombigbee River.[212]

At 3:00 a.m. on April 6, a bugle splits the still darkness with reveille, rousing the men from their slumbers. After the usual morning preliminaries, Boots and Saddles blares out, sending Croxton's brigade to their mounts. At about five o'clock in the morning, as the horsemen begin their southward trek, there is no way for them to know what a long and difficult day this will become. "The hardest day's march I think I ever made," remembers one young trooper from Michigan. Their first indication of trouble comes about twelve miles down the road at a huge gristmill on the banks of the Sipsey River, known as Lanier's and Jordan's Sipsey Mills. Here, Union scouts report that a large force of Forrest's cavalry, about three thousand strong, is on the west bank of the Tombigbee River and moving north toward them. Croxton also learns that Wilson has taken Selma, and Forrest has fled across the Cahaba River to the town of Marion. Knowing that his commander will no longer be needing him at Selma and feeling somewhat edgy over the presence of such a large force of Rebels coming their way, Croxton scraps his first plan and reverses his course, ordering a forced march back to Northport and Tuscaloosa.[213]

John Croxton's decision to avoid a fight with the Rebel force coming his way is not because of a lack of courage. The tall and lanky Croxton has been involved in nearly every battle in the western theater from Perryville to Nashville, and his superiors have eulogized him as "the dashing and gallant Croxton." But now he realizes he must be prudent in all his decisions, especially those that will affect the safety of his brigade. The young Yale graduate (class of 1857) must now use his head to not only accomplish the goals of the campaign but also make sure his men escape from this hostile country and rejoin the corps. So, before beginning his retreat back to Tuscaloosa, he takes the time to order the looting and burning of the gristmill on the Sipsey River. It is, after all, a military target, grinding about sixty thousand bushels of corn and wheat per year and serving as a Confederate commissary depot.[214]

The scouting reports telling Croxton that a force from Forrest's cavalry is moving his way will prove correct. That force is a brigade from Chalmers's division composed of Mississippi and Alabama men under the command of Wirt Adams. Wirt is an older brother of Daniel W. Adams, who had fought alongside Forrest at Selma. Formerly a planter, banker and politician, the Mississippian and his brigade have spent the early days of this last campaign guarding the Mobile and Ohio Railroad in and around Columbus, Mississippi. But after Wilson took Selma, Richard Taylor has ordered Adams to rejoin Forrest, who is now at Marion, Alabama, trying to collect the pieces of his scattered command. However, on April 5, the day Adams leaves Columbus and begins riding for Marion, Taylor becomes aware of Croxton's brigade moving southwest out of Tuscaloosa. Soon the telegraph lines are humming as Taylor gets word to Adams to "find and fight that column,"[215]

Wirt Adams wastes no time spurring his command to catch up with Croxton. Although now forty-six years old, Adams is still a fighter; at the beginning of the war, he had declined Jefferson Davis's offer to the position of postmaster general in favor of taking a field command. It didn't take long for him to establish himself as "one of the most dauntless cavalry leaders of the war." One admirer not only described the general as "handsome" but also lionized him with the melodramatic remark: "He stood six feet in his stirrups, the noblest paladin of the South who rode to war."[216]

Whether or not Adams is such a champion will remain, at best, an opinion. What is clear, however, is that he seems determined to find and fight Croxton's brigade. Thus, on April 6 at about noon, he and his horsemen see the smoke rising from the burning mill on the Sipsey River, revealing the presence of the Union cavalrymen. This happens to be the rear guard of Croxton's column, the Sixth Kentucky Cavalry, still waiting at the mill. The Kentucky Yankees are apparently expecting any approaching cavalry to be William Sutherland's company returning from its mission to Columbus, Mississippi. Hence, they are totally surprised when the leading column of Adams's brigade crashes into them. The result is nothing less than complete bedlam as wild-eyed Mississippians fire into the bluecoats, killing or capturing a number of them and sending the rest retreating to the brigade's supply train, which is about two miles down the Columbus Stage Road.[217]

The supply train is standing in an open field with no cover. Two ambulance wagons and Croxton's baggage wagon are there, along with a large herd of mules and horses confiscated from the farms they had passed. Milling about

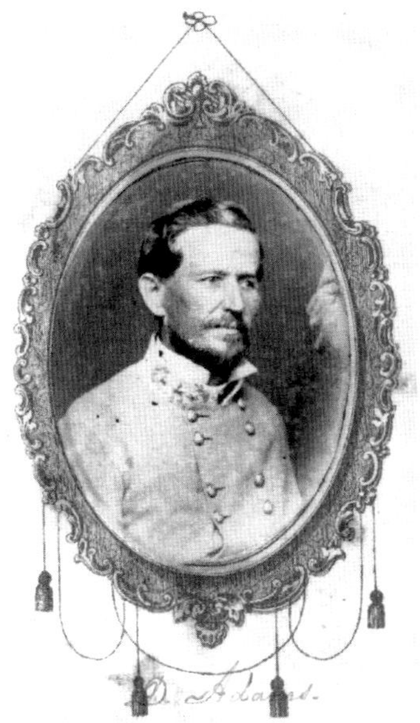

Confederate general Wirt Adams. *Courtesy Alabama Department of Archives and History, Montgomery, Alabama.*

the wagons are about sixty frantic slaves who have left their plantations and joined the Union column. Major William Fidler, the commanding officer of the Sixth Kentucky, scurries to organize his scattered troops into a defensive line around these wagons. The Kentuckians, now dismounted, hurriedly pull down stacks of cured bacon off the ambulances that were stolen from the mill and pile them up for cover to fight behind. By now, it's one o'clock, and Adams has assembled his Mississippians into a line of battle poised to attack the train. It's also about this time that the rain begins to fall, a driving downpour that will last the rest of the day.[218]

Charging through the rain, Adams's Confederates slam into the Union line. The fighting is fierce in places, with some of it becoming hand-to-hand. Fidler, sensing a disaster, scribbles out a note to the commander of the nearby Second Michigan Cavalry asking for help. But before the courier can leave with the message, Fidler falls from his horse, and his 150 Kentuckians are routed by the oncoming Rebels. Those not killed or wounded begin running for the safety of the brigade, leaving behind the slaves, animals and wagons—one of the wagons contains Croxton's personal belongings. But in the confusion and pelting rain, some of the men, including Fidler, lose their sense of direction and wander into the woods or veer off into Sipsey Swamp.[219]

Strung out for miles, the Kentuckians and their Rebel pursuers are running north through the thunderous storm. The Second Michigan Cavalry is the next body of troops in Croxton's column, positioned across the road on the edge of a field bracing for the Rebel attack. One Michigan soldier watching the Kentucky Yankees running wildly for their lives is prompted to make a critical remark about his compatriots in his next home letter. "They have behaved in a disgraceful manner," he contends. Then, as if by design, the moment the retreating Kentuckians approach the safety of the Michigan line, it parts just long enough to let them through and then closes again as Adams's mounted troops charge toward the bluecoats. By now, it's midafternoon, with rain pouring from a dark sky, and the Spencer carbines of the Michigan men open up, turning back the Rebel charge. At the same time, several companies of the Eighth Iowa Cavalry suddenly appear on the flank to reinforce the Michigan regiment.[220]

But the Rebel general, Wirt Adams, has no intention of giving up. He orders his Mississippians and Alabamans to dismount and charge across the field, which by now has turned into a morass of mud from the hundreds of horses stomping through it during the rainy afternoon. Three times the Confederates throw themselves through the rain and mud against the Union line. And although the Michigan regiment holds its ground, the Iowa soldiers on the flank eventually break under the relentless Rebel onslaughts, scattering into the woods. Adams, for some reason, does not take advantage of the collapsed flank and ceases attacking after the third charge. During the lull, the Michigan troops see their chance to withdraw and quickly do so. Adams continues pursuing them into the blinding rainstorm until the Union rear guard falls back into a swamp near the town of Romulus and darkness prevents any further pursuit.[221]

The next morning, April 7, Adams sends out a group of scouts to determine Croxton's position and movement. The scout's first sighting happens to be some Yankee foraging parties, moving northwest along the Columbus Road. Mistaking them to be a part of Croxton's main body, the scouts then report this to Adams. The Rebel commander naturally assumes that Croxton is now moving to Columbus to destroy the Mobile and Ohio Railroad. Reacting to his scouts' fallacious information, he orders his men to mount up for a forced march that will take them a grueling forty-five miles in eleven hours. After arriving in Columbus, Adams realizes his mistake. He's been innocently duped by his own scouts. What's more, Croxton is actually moving east toward Tuscaloosa, in the opposite direction, leaving Adams at least seventy miles away. Any hopes of catching him now have vanished. The chase is over.[222]

The running fight between Croxton and Adams on April 6 is generally considered a Confederate victory and, in fact, the last of the Confederate victories on Alabama soil during the war. But John Croxton did not agree with any such conclusion, not officially at least. His reports contended that the twenty-three-mile running fight was really nothing more than a slight skirmish with his rear guard. Also, his statement that his losses amounted to 36, which included 2 officers, does not agree with other documented figures. Those sources estimate his casualties to be at least 76 men, most of whom were captured. Finally, his contention that his rear guard was "molested" by two brigades under Adams numbering almost 3,000 is an obvious fabrication. Actually, the two sides were about evenly matched, each having nearly 1,500 cavalrymen. It's also clear that the Rebel horsemen did drive the bluecoats out of Pickens County, Alabama, and away from their intended target of the Alabama and Mississippi Railroad. So it seems that the Confederates under Adams somehow achieved a victory with inferior weapons, equipment and animals and, at the same time, incurred only half the losses of their enemy.[223]

Regardless of how many losses Croxton suffered during the long day of April 6, two of those losses were especially painful for him. First was the loss of Captain William Sutherland, who was not only Croxton's assistant adjutant general but also one of his favorite and most reliable staff officers. After being sent on a special mission to Columbus, Mississippi, with twenty-five troopers from the Sixth Kentucky Cavalry to mislead the enemy into believing that city was the next target on Croxton's list, Sutherland was supposed to rejoin the brigade at a point on the Tombigbee River. But after Adams's Confederate brigade arrived in the vicinity, Sutherland soon found the whole countryside to be infested with Rebel cavalrymen, preventing him from safely returning to Croxton's brigade. With no other choice, he took his command north, all the way to Decatur, Alabama, resulting in his absence for the remainder of the campaign.[224]

Croxton's most serious loss, however, was Major William Fidler, regimental commander of the Sixth Kentucky Cavalry. During the running fight of April 6, Fidler and two of his troopers were somehow separated from the regiment. Wandering blindly through the woods and swamps during that stormy afternoon, they lost their sense of direction. Eventually, the three found themselves on the land of John D. Horton, a wealthy planter and "ardent Southern sympathizer." When Horton discovered the presence of Yankees hiding in his swamp, he gathered up his "fine pack of trained hounds," normally used to pursue runaway slaves, and turned them loose on Fidler and his men. The hounds had no trouble picking up their trail, and soon Horton, with the help of the local militia, captured the Yankee runners.[225]

For Fidler, being taken prisoner was certainly unfortunate but hardly the end of his woes. After being escorted to the Eutaw jail, he and his men were

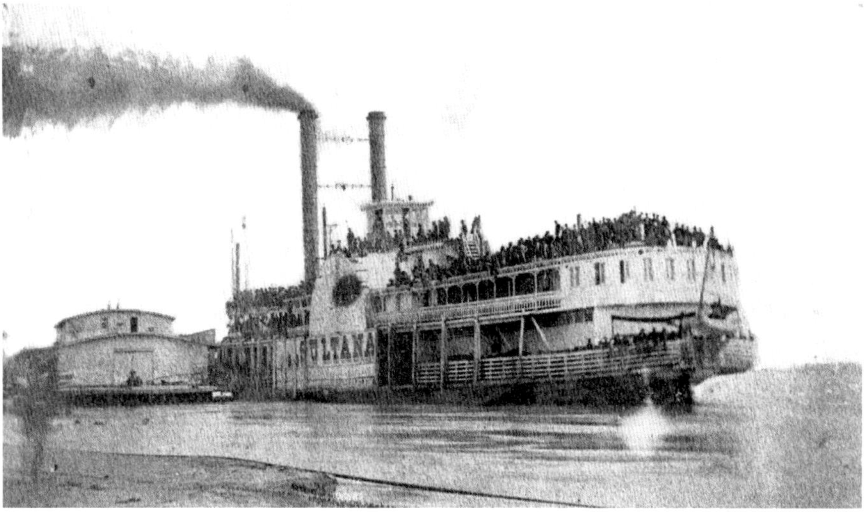

The steamer *Sultana*. *Courtesy Library of Congress.*

sent on to a prison camp in Meridian, Mississippi. With the war all but over, he was released on April 21, and on April 27, he boarded the steamer *Sultana* at Vicksburg, along with 1,700 freed Union prisoners and discharged soldiers. The boat was dangerously overloaded, and three of its four boilers exploded just north of Memphis in the worst maritime disaster in American history. The death toll of soldiers was estimated at 1,585. And Fidler was among them.[226]

By Friday night, April 7, Croxton is back in Northport. For the next four days, the brigade stays around the Northport-Tuscaloosa area, much to the chagrin of the local population, who had hoped they had seen the last of the Yankee raiders. They had already stripped the land clean of food and fodder from their first visit here, and Croxton would not have remained in the barren area except for the purpose of waiting on William Sutherland and his scouts to return. Sutherland, of course, never returns, and Croxton rides out of Tuscaloosa County on April 12. He decides on an eastward destination, toward Elyton, where he hopes to learn something of the whereabouts of the corps and, with luck, open communications with Wilson.[227]

After leaving the town of Jasper, the Lost Brigade is forced into taking on an amphibious character. Because of the nearly constant spring rains, they must spend a great deal of time crossing the flooded rivers, streams and creeks of the twin forks of the Black Warrior River. Since so many of the bridges have been destroyed, many of these waters are crossed by swimming or by ferry boat. There are, of course, the usual reports of men and animals drowning. One comes from twenty-two-year-old Charles Wooster, who comes dangerously close to going into a watery grave. "In crossing one of these rivers it was my fortune to have the boat capsize just as it was pushing out from shore." Loaded down with his Spencer carbine, his saber and fifty rounds of ammunition, Wooster is nearly swept under. In a letter to his brother, he explains his close encounter: "I found it slightly inconvenient to keep my nose above water until I could get hold of a little sapling which was nearby." Besides the perils of nearly drowning, Wooster and his comrades must deal with other problems along the way. Food, for example, is hard to come by in this part of the country. Their rations have long since been devoured. The hilly land here is miles north of the rich Black Belt, and there are very few farms along the way. Of the farms they do pass, there is little to confiscate since, as Wooster says, "The people were generally poor."[228]

Once over the forks of the Black Warrior, Croxton and his horsemen ride into Mt. Pinson late on April 19. Here, for the first time, they learn that Wilson has left Selma after defeating Forrest and then taken Montgomery and moved east toward Georgia. Having a good idea of Wilson's location and destination, Croxton, at last, is sure of his own course. He knows, however, that course will be difficult. Although his brigade has continually met and talked with Confederate deserters, stragglers and paroled prisoners during their journey, there has been no official word of a truce or surrender, and they are still in hostile country defended by Rebel soldiers. What's more, his men are low on ammunition. Before leaving Mt. Pinson, he orders the destruction of the foundry and niter works located there.[229]

Moving on, the brigade reaches the unfordable Coosa River at Talladega on April 22. Crossing it by ferry, Croxton learns that there is yet another enemy force ahead of him at Blue Mountain Station. This one is led by a recently appointed general named Benjamin Jefferson Hill, formerly the provost marshal of the Army of Tennessee. Hill's brigade supposedly numbers about five hundred men, but there are few, if any, veterans among them. They are, for the most part, a motley lot of local home guards and a few state militiamen who are clearly not interested in fighting a veteran Yankee cavalry brigade three times their size. Thus, by the time Croxton's horsemen reach them on the twenty-fouth, all but about one hundred of these reluctant men have disappeared into the woods, and those remaining are easily routed. Scoffing at their feckless stand, a Michigan cavalryman offers this insulting remark: "The Rebels would brake as often as they were charged, and they were charged as often as they stood." With Hill's weak defense disposed of, Croxton orders the Blue Mountain station burned, tears up the bridges on the Alabama and Tennessee River Railroad and leaves the nearby Oxford Iron Company Furnace in flames.[230]

The next day, April 25, the Lost Brigade leaves Alabama and crosses the state line into Georgia. By now the men know that the main corps is in Macon, and in a few days they will join them. They also know that the war is about over. During this last leg of their journey, they have continued to pass the ragged gray coats from Lee's Army of Northern Virginia limping down the roads toward their homes. While Croxton naturally suspects that the war is over, he's still unsure. The next day, when they cross the Chattahoochee River at Newnan, Georgia, a flag of truce is waving, and Croxton is told by Rebel authorities there that an armistice between Sherman and Johnston has already been signed. But in the absence of official notification from his superiors, Croxton fails to recognize the truce and keeps his horsemen moving. According to Wilson, he gravely tells the Southerners he "would trouble nobody who kept out of his way."[231]

At last, on May 1, 1865, more than a month after leaving Wilson and the corps at Elyton, Croxton and the Lost Brigade ride into Macon, Georgia. For them, their 653-mile journey through Dixie has been a long and difficult one. Although Wilson will later say, "The story of his [Croxton's] march reads like a romance of chivalry," the people of Alabama would most likely disagree. All they can see is that he and his raiders have destroyed "five iron works, three factories, numerous mills and immense quantities of supplies." Now that Croxton is reunited with Wilson, the young cavalry general can add these to the damage and destruction the main corps has caused the Confederacy's military production.[232]

Without a doubt, Wilson can look back on the trail of destruction he has left behind on his rampage through the heartland of the Confederacy and know that he has struck a blow from which the South can never recover. The munition and iron industry in Alabama, so vital to the Confederate war effort, is now lying in ruins. And there is a shadow of misery as Wilson and his raiders ride out of the state. The South seems suddenly doomed, not only with the defeat of Forrest and the surrender of the armies of Lee and Johnston but also with the assassination of Lincoln and what it must endure in the years after defeat.

Chapter 12

"God's Will Be Done"

By the time Wilson reunites his corps on May 1, 1865, hostilities have ended and so, too, has his legendary military campaign, which will soon bear the name "Wilson's Raid." There is, however, one final task that lies ahead of him. Secretary of War Edwin Stanton has issued an order to Wilson and other commanders instructing them on government policies following the surrender, as well as further directing them to "pursue and capture the Confederate chiefs who might be trying to escape from the country." These would include such important leaders as Jefferson Davis, Alexander Stephens and Judah Benjamin, as well as a host of other bureaucrats who have fled Richmond and are rumored to be making their way south through the Carolinas and Georgia to some point where they can continue the resistance. Wilson has long since suspected this and wastes no time in dispatching nearly everyone from his headquarters in Macon to move across the entire state of Georgia, casting a huge dragnet to trap the Confederate fugitives. Then, as a further incentive to spur his men in their search, Wilson exceeds his authority and offers a reward of $500,000 for the capture of the Confederate president. Such a motivation naturally stimulates the troops to the point where Wilson later acknowledges that "[e]very officer and man was anxious to assist in the capture of Davis and his party."[233]

Wilson's belief about the direction Davis is moving proves to be correct. In fact, the Confederate president and his party have been quietly moving along the back roads, passing through the piney woods of Georgia for several days.

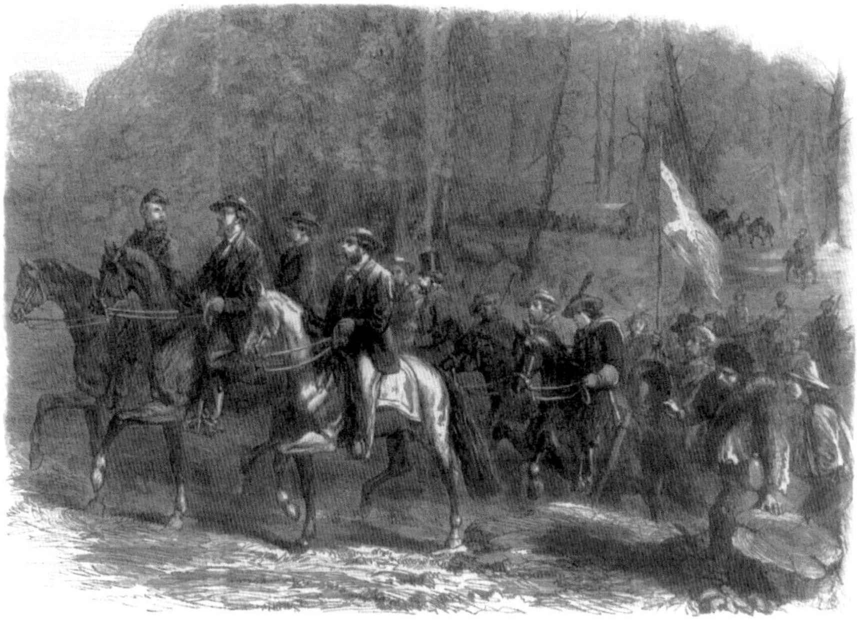

Jefferson Davis (*second from left*) accompanied by some of his cabinet members in flight through Georgia shortly before their capture. *Courtesy Library of Congress.*

By May 9, they have reached the vicinity of Irwinville in the southern part of the state. And it's here that two of Wilson's best units, the First Wisconsin from Croxton's brigade and the Fourth Michigan from Robert Minty's command, are closing in on them. Through some miscommunication, however, the two units are unaware of each other's presence or position as they approach the Davis campsite in the predawn hours of May 10. Of course, the sleeping Southerners are not aware of the three hundred Federals creeping through the woods toward them. Just before dawn, they are awakened by rifle shots ringing out about one hundred yards from their camp. However, the shots are not from their sentries, but from the two Yankee units that have accidentally collided in the thick pines and opened fire on each other. This arouses the camp, and Davis's black coachman, James Jones, seeing the cavalrymen surrounding the camp, yells out a warning that the Yankees have come.[234]

So rapid is the surprise invasion of the camp that not a shot is fired by the party of Confederates. Even those who do manage to draw their pistols, such as Davis's aide, Colonel William Preston Johnston, and John Reagan, the postmaster general, immediately realize that their resistance would be pointless and surrender their weapons. Two more of Davis's aides,

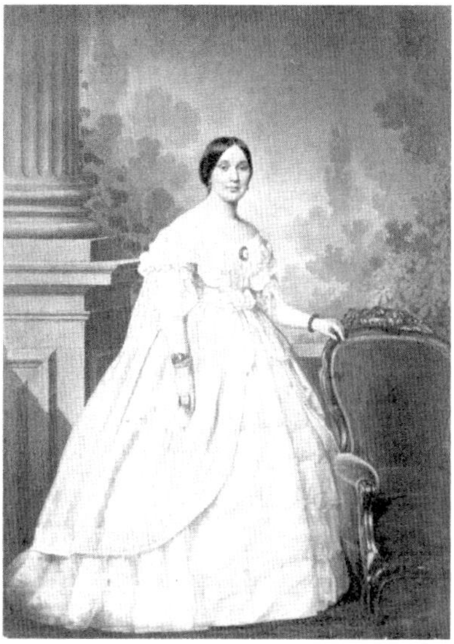

Varina Davis, "First Lady of the Confederacy." *Courtesy Library of Congress.*

John Wood and Francis Lubbock, try to mount their horses and escape, but neither is able to get into the saddle before being stopped.

At first, the tents and their occupants are not disturbed. Some distance away, at the Davis family tent, the president, who has slept in his clothes, hears all the commotion and gunshots. Pulling on his boots and throwing back the tent flaps, he steps outside into a drizzling rain, where, through the dim morning light, he can make out the attackers as Yankee soldiers. Quickly ducking back into the tent, he tells his wife, Varina, "It is the Federal cavalry and they are on us." Then aide John Wood runs to the Davis tent unobserved and tells the president there may be time for him to escape in the confusion, pointing out a creek bottom in the opposite direction. Varina agrees with Wood, and both begin urging Davis to flee while there's still time.[235]

But the president dithers. He fears for Varina and their children. And he has never been one to run from a fight. As precious seconds are ticking away, a lone Yankee approaches the tent. Varina walks boldly toward the soldier, Corporal George Munger, telling him there are no men in the tent, only women and children, and asks for privacy. At the same time, Burton Harrison, the president's private secretary, appears and begins walking with Munger, leading him away from the tent and distracting him with conversation. Inside the tent, Davis finally submits to his wife's wishes and reaches for his overcoat as he prepares to leave. In the dark tent, he mistakenly picks up Varina's gray raglan cloak. Worried that he will be recognized Varina runs after him and throws her shawl over his head and shoulders. So, with no intention of disguising himself as such, Davis nevertheless now appears to be a woman as he walks toward the creek bottom.[236]

The shroud and veil almost work until Corporal Munger happens to look back and sees someone quietly slipping away from the tent toward the forest. Even though Varina has assured him that only women and children were in the tent, Munger knows that a woman would not be wearing boots and spurs and yells at Davis to halt. Mounting his horse, he rides toward him, raising his carbine, cocking the hammer and pointing it at the president. Two more soldiers on horseback then appear, and Varina loses her composure and runs to her husband, throws her arms around his neck and cries out, "Don't shoot." This, of course, ends Davis's attempt to escape, and he follows Munger back to the tent, mumbling in an undertone, "God's will be done."[237]

Although Corporal Munger claims to recognize his prisoner as Jefferson Davis, the man's identity is still not certain. Half an hour later, Benjamin Pritchard and Henry Harnden, the colonels commanding the two Yankee regiments, ride into the camp. Dismounting, Pritchard introduces himself and Harnden to the prisoners gathered before him. Davis then steps forward and asks Pritchard if he commands these men. "Yes," answers Pritchard, and he asks what he should call the man addressing him. The president, in a moment of petulance, replies, "You may call me whom you are a mind to." Pritchard, then sure that this must be his man, says, "Well then, I will call you Davis." After a moment, the president replies, "Yes, I am President Davis."[238]

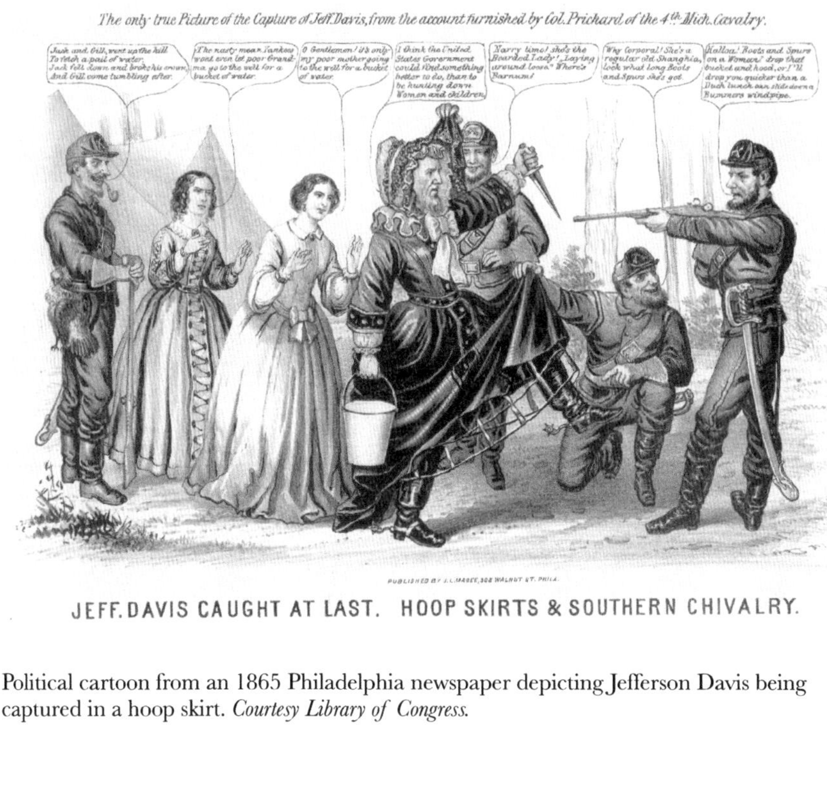

Political cartoon from an 1865 Philadelphia newspaper depicting Jefferson Davis being captured in a hoop skirt. *Courtesy Library of Congress.*

News of the capture of Jefferson Davis and his party reaches Wilson on May 12 while the Wisconsin and Michigan cavalrymen are still escorting them to his headquarters in Macon. The next day they arrive. Included in the captured party are President Davis; his wife, Varina Davis; her sister, Margaret Howell; four children; Postmaster General John Reagan; Davis's aides, Colonels Preston Johnston and Francis Lubbock; Davis's secretary, Colonel Burton Harrison; four junior officers; thirteen enlisted men; and several black servants and teamsters.[239]

Even though the capture of Jefferson Davis is a significant postwar achievement for the "Boy General," it certainly isn't the only one. During this same time, units from Wilson's command also apprehend a number of other Confederate bureaucrats and high-ranking military men. Vice President Alexander Stephens is arrested at his plantation in Crawfordville, Georgia, and in LaGrange, Georgia, Secretary of the Navy Stephen R. Mallory and Senator Benjamin Hill are taken into custody. The Rebel cavalry general "Fighting Joe" Wheeler is also taken prisoner by Wilson's raiders, as is the governor of Georgia, Joseph E. Brown. In fact, the only Southerners who succeed in slipping through Wilson's net are Davis's closest confidant in the cabinet, Secretary of State Judah P. Benjamin; Secretary of War John C. Breckenridge; and Robert Toombs, a former secretary of state. But all in all, Wilson is pleased with both his campaign and the capture of Davis and so many of the Confederate fugitives and never hesitates to sing the praises of himself and his raiders: "Our task was done and done well."[240]

Following his victory at Selma, Wilson had naturally assumed that sooner or later, Nathan Bedford Forrest would come after him. But he doesn't. After being defeated at Selma, Forrest knows his cavalry is too small, too battered and too disheartened to have any real effect at stopping such a large force. Any attempt at doing so would only be a needless sacrifice of his troops. Besides, after Wilson leaves Montgomery moving east, it's apparent that he's leaving Alabama, which is Forrest's responsibility to defend, and entering Georgia, where Wilson will be Howell Cobb's problem. So, by mid-April, Forrest is in Gainesville, Alabama, a small town sitting on a bluff on the west side of the Tombigbee River. From here he will try to gather as many troops as possible, remount them and mold them into enough of a fighting force that they can keep defending their homeland.

Throughout the month of April, rumors are running wild among his troops. Some of them, Forrest learns, are true. For instance, by the middle of the month, the fall of Mobile and Lee's surrender to Grant have been verified by his superior, Richard Taylor. But other news—such as Johnston's surrender, Lincoln's assassination and Jefferson Davis and the Confederate government fleeing southward to continue the war—has not yet been confirmed. Thus, without official notification of these things, Forrest has no choice but to continue preparing to fight the enemy. As for the rumors, Forrest issues an order to his soldiers on April 25, stating in part, "No credence should be given to such reports: nor should they for a moment control the actions or influence the feelings, sentiments, or conduct of the troops of this command." Forrest is still not completely convinced that the Confederacy is falling apart and continues his charge to the men: "It is the duty of every man to stand firm at his post and true to his colors." Then, as if admitting that the dreadful news might prove to be true, he tells them, "A few days more will determine the truth or falsity of all the reports now in circulation."[241]

The rumors of the Confederacy collapsing are, of course, true. And the bad news keeps coming. On the last day of April, Forrest is notified that Richard Taylor has agreed to surrender all the forces under his command to General Canby. For Forrest, a man unaccustomed to defeat even in the face of impossible odds, the news is hard to accept. Many, in fact, are wondering if a man such as Forrest will ever surrender. And many of his veteran troops urge him to lead them west of the Mississippi to continue the struggle. Such talk begins to fuel speculation among the Federal generals as to what Forrest plans to do.

Among those who are worried that Forrest will continue to fight is Sherman, who writes his wife, Ellen, on April 29, the same day Taylor surrenders: "There is great danger of the Confederate armies breaking up into guerillas and that is what I fear most. Such men as Wade Hampton, Forrest, Wirt Adams…never will work and their Negroes are all gone, their plantations destroyed, &c." And expressing the same sentiment to Grant, Sherman writes, "I now apprehend that the rebel armies will disperse and…we will have to deal with numberless bands of desperadoes, headed by such men as Mosby, Forrest, Red Jackson, and others, who know not and care not for danger or its consequences."[242]

Another Federal general who is apprehensive over the future plans of Forrest is George Thomas. In fact, Thomas has received a disturbing report from one of his subordinates in the field that Forrest is already planning to lead his men into Texas or Mexico and carry on the war from there. Apparently, he has such confidence in this report that he answers, "Send under flag of truce, a summons to Forrest to surrender upon the terms given by General Grant to Generals Lee and Johnston. Inform him, at the same time, of the rumors which have reached you, and that you are prepared for him, and if he attempts such a reckless and bloodthirsty adventure he will be treated thereafter as an outlaw, and the states of Mississippi and Alabama will be so destroyed that they will not recover for fifty years."[243]

Although there is some evidence that Forrest entertained the idea of going west and continuing the struggle, it was never a serious consideration. Forrest is and always has been a realist. He has no intention of risking anymore of his men's lives chasing a hopeless cause. Besides, Forrest is nearly forty-four years old, and he's been in the saddle for four long years, fighting in all kinds of conditions, and bears the scars of four bullet wounds. In short, he's worn out. Although he rarely speaks of what he intends to do since the South surrendered, he minces no words with two politicians who pay him a visit on May 3 following Taylor's surrender. Mississippi governor Charles Clark and Isham Harris, a former governor of Tennessee, begin presenting to him their plan of going to Texas and joining Confederates there who are still fighting. Before they can finish, Forrest interrupts. "Men," he snaps, "you may all do as you damn please, but I'm a-going home." Harris, however, refuses to take no for an answer and keeps imploring the general to continue leading his men in battle. But well aware of the futility of such a venture, Forrest retorts, "To make men fight under such circumstances would be nothing but murder." Then he adds one final admonition: "Any man who is in favor of a further prosecution of this war is a fit subject for a lunatic asylum."[244]

Convincing his men to submit in the face of what has become a hopeless fight is another matter. Many of them, especially the younger ones, are stunned by the surrender and heartbroken over the prospect of giving up their struggle for independence. Boyish-looking John Morton, barely twenty-one and Forrest's chief of artillery, is especially upset over the outcome. Consoling him, Forrest says, "You are young, John, and you will soon get over it all. Go home and study medicine with your father. It is a noble and grand profession, and I shall love to think of you as being of service to your fellow men in that way." Still, some of them vow never to surrender and plead with Forrest to take them west of the Mississippi and continue the war. "No," he tells them. "What couldn't be accomplished here could never be done in the thinly settled west." After reasoning with them, they finally accept the idea of returning to their homes. One regiment, the Seventh Tennessee Cavalry, gathers around its silk flag and conducts a reverent ceremony. The flag has always been something special to the men, a gift from a young woman in Aberdeen, Mississippi, made from her wedding dress. Cutting the banner into strips, each man takes one as a token of their long struggle.[245]

But this is not the only memento they will carry with them. On the morning of May 9, the day of the formal surrender, Forrest summons his assistant adjutant, Charles Anderson, the same man who had accompanied him to the prisoner exchange meeting in Mississippi with Union officers back in February. He asks Anderson to take a horseback ride with him through the countryside. At first, they ride in silence, and it's apparent to Anderson that the general is in a sorrowful mood. Finally, Forrest opens up, expressing to his adjutant his deep regret about surrendering and even admitting that he had entertained thoughts of going to Mexico. But his mind is made up: "I will share the fate of my men." And he asks Anderson to prepare an address to his troops, just as the adjutant has done so many times during the war. They continue to talk, and Forrest, in his homely manner, explains what he wants the document to say. Anderson, of course, is Forrest's wordsmith, and the unpolished general depends on him to take his thoughts and articulate them to his men in all the eloquence of the King's English. And this he does, writing the speech on the top of a cracker box, then setting the words in type and running it off on a printing press so that each soldier could have a copy. Thanks to Forrest's strong feelings for his men and Anderson's literary talents, this farewell document could arguably be the most powerful peacemaking one ever given by a Confederate commander at a surrender.[246]

He begins the address with the inescapable truth: "That we are beaten is a self-evident fact, and any further resistance on our part would be justly regarded as the very height of folly and rashness….The cause for which you have so long and manfully struggled, and for which you have braved dangers, endured privations and sufferings, and made so many sacrifices, is today hopeless."

Forrest then turns to the business of duty and reconciliation: "It is your duty and mine to lay down our arms, submit to the 'powers that be,' and to aid in restoring the peace and establishing law and order throughout the land….Civil War, such as you have just passed through, naturally engenders feelings of animosity, hatred and revenge. It is our duty to divest ourselves of all such feelings, and, so far as it is in our power to do so, to cultivate friendly feelings toward those with whom we have so long contested, and heretofore so widely but honestly differed."

Finally, "Old Bedford" charts a future course for his men, giving them one last order: "You have been good soldiers, you can be good citizens. Obey the laws, preserve your honor, and the government to which you have surrendered can afford to be and will be magnanimous."

Analysis

There is little doubt among most historians that Wilson's Raid served as the final death blow to the Confederate States of America. Its importance, however, did not derive solely from a military standpoint. From that perspective, the South was already on its knees by the time Wilson crossed the Tennessee River and rode into Alabama in 1865. Rather, the significance of the campaign lies primarily in the fact that the destruction of the Confederacy's last war manufacturing centers in the heartland of the South left it unable to carry on the rebellion east of the Mississippi. In fact, the trail of destruction was so complete that when it was over every blast furnace in Alabama except one had been razed, leaving the iron industry virtually dead. And the raiders' destruction did not stop there. Along with the loss of the iron production, the South was deprived of factories, foundries, warehouses, gun and ammunition arsenals, shipyards, railroad cars and anything that could possibly be used in its war effort.[247]

Credit for the thoroughness of the destruction—assuming an aptitude for burning and tearing up things is to be considered commendable—clearly belongs to James H. Wilson. The young general was among the best at prosecuting war in a deliberate fashion—much like a businessman at work. He knew that his objective was to wreck anything of military value that stood in his path, and this he successfully accomplished. It was largely made possible because of what his biographer, Edward Longacre, pointed out as one of his strongest character traits: "a longstanding urge to succeed at all cost."[248]

But Wilson's zeal for accomplishing this mission often carried him outside the boundaries of a military operation. In the wake of his raid, he left a trail littered with the unnecessary destruction of civilian property. What's more, there were clearly many incidents of looting and heinous behavior by his men against civilians. There is, of course, no evidence that he ordered any nonmilitary targets destroyed, and he certainly never encouraged or authorized his troops to plunder the assets of civilians. In fact, the opposite is true, as orders were circulated among his cavalry on several occasions during the mission that private property should be spared. But Wilson, much like Sherman during his March to the Sea, silently tolerated his soldiers' bad behavior as an inevitable byproduct of war. When it came to the success of the mission, both men, after all, were pragmatists in the first sense of the word. Yet, in any comparison of the two campaigns, it should be noted that the devastation left by Sherman far exceeded anything in Wilson's path. As historian James Pickett Jones correctly pointed out, "The cavalry corps was far smaller than Sherman's army, and discipline was easier to maintain. Besides, Wilson's horsemen moved too rapidly to linger and plunder." Also, it should be remembered that cities along Wilson's march, such as Montgomery and Tuskegee, that offered no defense fared much better in terms of civilian destruction, compared to those like Selma that tried to resist. And in that vein, Confederate leaders such as Jefferson Davis, Judah Benjamin and Alabama governor Thomas Watts must at least share in the blame for much of the destruction of Wilson's Raid for refusing to recognize in those final months of the war that they could not win what couldn't possibly be won.[249]

From a strictly military perspective, Wilson's accomplishments were not so much in the victories he achieved against a greatly inferior enemy but for his excellent use of cavalry. With the exception of Wirt Adams's victory over Croxton, Wilson's raiders easily defeated the cavalry of Forrest in every engagement. But as General Grant pointed out in his memoirs, "Forrest was in his [Wilson's] front, but with neither his old-time army nor his old-time prestige. He now had principally conscripts. His conscripts were generally old men and boys."[250]

Notwithstanding all of Forrest's disadvantages, it's unlikely that even he, the "Wizard of the Saddle," could have succeeded in defeating Wilson had their numbers and experience been comparable. And this can only be attributed to Wilson's insight as to how to organize, move and engage a large body of cavalry. Moreover, he was a man who exceeded his time in terms of having an understanding of cavalry as an antecedent to mechanized infantry. The only difference, as historian Bruce Catton pointed out, was that Wilson depended on hay-fed horses to move his army swiftly from place to place, whereas true mechanized infantry, in the modern sense, relies on gasoline-powered machinery. While their means of transportation clearly differed, their tactics—in theory at least—were the same. Germany's blitzkrieg, or lightning warfare, of World War II comes to mind as an example of a large-scale military force striking with a sudden, swift and concentrated effort to achieve a rapid victory. Of course, Forrest also understood the use of cavalry in this same sense and used it to achieve victory in nearly all of his engagements. But in this campaign, Wilson clearly got the best of Forrest at the very game he had perfected and even named with the simple phrase "Get there first with the most men." Perhaps Catton summed it up best when he wrote, "When Wilson finished reequipping and reorganizing he would have 12,000 superbly mounted men, all of them armed with repeating rifles and trained to fight on foot; they had more firepower than an infantry corps, they could move much faster than any infantry, and there was nothing in the South that could stop them."[251]

Notes

Chapter 1

1. Henry, *"First with the Most" Forrest*, 423; Jones, *Yankee Blitzkrieg*, 22–24. Although he wore the wreathed three stars of a lieutenant general during the meeting, Forrest's commission to that rank was not actually official until February 28.
2. Henry, *"First with the Most" Forrest*, 423.
3. Wilson, *Under the Old Flag*, 46.
4. U.S. War Department, *War of the Rebellion*, ser. 1, vol. 38, pt. 4, 480. Hereafter, this source will be cited as *OR*, and all references being to series 1 unless otherwise indicated. Whenever a volume consists of two or more parts, the volume number will precede the *OR* followed by the part number and page number; Hosea, "Some Side Lights," 9–15.
5. Wilson, *Under the Old Flag*, 46; Hosea, "Some Side Lights."
6. Wilson, *Under the Old Flag*, 46; Forrest quoted in Henry, *"First with the Most" Forrest*, 424; Jones, *Yankee Blitzkrieg*, 24–25.
7. Henry, *"First with the Most" Forrest*, 423; Wilson, *Under the Old Flag*, 46. Forrest's ban on using sabers does not include officers, who continue to be armed with them throughout the war.
8. Wilson, *Under the Old Flag*, 46; Hosea, "Some Side Lights."
9. Hurst, *Nathan Bedford Forrest*, 247; Henry, *"First with the Most" Forrest*, 424–25; Hosea, "Some Side Lights."
10. 49 *OR* 1, 355; Jones, *Yankee Blitzkrieg*, 19, 38.

11. Longacre, *From Union Stars to Top Hat*, 197–98; Jones, *Yankee Blitzkrieg*, 13–14; Wilson, *Under the Old Flag*, 46; 49 *OR* 1, 342, 355.
12. Longacre, *From Union Stars to Top Hat*, 22, 152–56.
13. Ibid., 27–35; Jones, *Yankee Blitzkrieg*, 3–8; Warner, *Generals in Blue*, 566–68.
14. Wilson, *Under the Old Flag*, 47.
15. Ibid.
16. Jones, *Yankee Blitzkrieg*, 16–19; Wilson, *Under the Old Flag*, 48; 49 *OR* 1, 356.
17. 49 *OR* 1, 356; Jones, *Yankee Blitzkrieg*, 20–21.
18. Wilson, *Under the Old Flag*, 47–48; Jones, *Yankee Blitzkrieg*, 28.

Chapter 2

19. Faust, *This Republic of Suffering*, 137–49, quoted in South Carolina newspaper *Daily South Carolinian*, page 149; Castel, *Decision in the West*, 20–27 (Confederate officer quoted on page 21).
20. Faust, *This Republic of Suffering*, 191–93; Wiley, *Life of Johnny Reb*, 308–14.
21. Taylor, *Destruction and Reconstruction*, 198–99; Warner, *Generals in Gray*, 299–300.
22. For some of the excellent sources drawn from describing the character and background of Nathan Bedford Forrest, see Wyeth, *That Devil Forrest*; Henry, *"First with the Most" Forrest*; Hurst, *Nathan Bedford Forrest*; Henry, *As They Saw Forrest.*
23. Wyeth, *That Devil Forrest*, xv–xxxviii, "War means fighting…," quoted on xxi; Taylor, *Destruction and Reconstruction*, 200.
24. Henry, *"First with the Most" Forrest*, 13; Hurst, *Nathan Bedford Forrest*, 6–7; Henry, *As They Saw Forrest*, xii.
25. Wyeth, *That Devil Forrest*, 554–78, conversation with widow quoted on page 556; Henry, *As They Saw Forrest*, 270 and 275.
26. Wyeth, *That Devil Forrest*, 570–71; Henry, *As They Saw Forrest*, 37; James Pickett Jones, *Yankee Blitzkrieg*, 43; 49 *OR* 1, 931.
27. Henry, *"First with the Most" Forrest*, 415.
28. 45 *OR* 2, 756; Hurst, *Nathan Bedford Forrest*, 245.
29. 45 *OR* 2, 622; conversation with officer quoted in Wyeth, *That Devil Forrest*, 511.
30. 45 *OR* 2, 758–59.
31. Warner, *Generals in Gray*, 46; conversation between Forrest and Chalmers quoted in Groom, *Shrouds of Glory*, 141.

32. 45 *OR* 2, 759; 45 *OR* 2, 751.
33. 45 *OR* 2, 751–52; Henry, *"First with the Most" Forrest*, 418; Henry, *As They Saw Forrest*, 211. There were exceptions to the furloughs, including Lawrence Ross's Texas Brigade, which simply had too far to travel, and Philip Roddey's Brigade, which remained on picket duty near the Tennessee River to watch and report on Wilson's threatening force.
34. Wyeth, *That Devil Forrest*, 514; Warner, *Generals in Gray*, 2–3, 12–13, 288; Evans, *Confederate Military History*, 235.
35. Warner, *Generals in Gray*, 25, 42, 152–53, 263–64; Henry, *"First with the Most" Forrest*, 422.
36. Henry, *"First with the Most" Forrest*, 422; Warner, *Generals in Gray*, 1, 39, 262.
37. Jones, *Yankee Blitzkrieg*, 48–50; Henry, *"First with the Most" Forrest*, 422–23.
38. Wyeth, *That Devil Forrest*, 516; Chalmers, "Forrest and His Campaigns," 485.
39. O'Brien, *Mobile, 1865*, 61; Jones, *Yankee Blitzkrieg*, 51–52.

Chapter 3

40. Wilson, *Under the Old Flag*, 42; Jones, *Yankee Blitzkrieg*, 30; Warner, *Generals in Blue*, 104, 296.
41. Wilson, *Under the Old Flag*, 42–43; Jones, *Yankee Blitzkrieg*, 31; Warner, *Generals in Blue*, 283.
42. Wilson, *Under the Old Flag*, 41–42; Warner, *Generals in Blue*, 519–20; Jones, *Yankee Blitzkrieg*, 32.
43. Jones, *Yankee Blitzkrieg*, 34–35; Wilson, *Under the Old Flag*, 48.
44. 49 *OR* 1, 356, 404; Longacre, "To Tuscaloosa and Beyond," 109–22; Wilson, *Under the Old Flag*, 48–49.
45. Gilpin, "Last Campaign," 630; Longacre, "To Tuscaloosa and Beyond," 112.
46. Longacre, *From Union Stars to Top Hat*, 202; Wilson, *Under the Old Flag*, 49; 49 *OR* 1, 404.
47. 49 *OR* 1, 405; 49 *OR* 2, 1,155, 1,160; Wilson, *Under the Old Flag*, 51.
48. 49 *OR* 1, 405; Longacre, "To Tuscaloosa and Beyond," 112; Gilpin, "Last Campaign," 631; Jones, *Yankee Blitzkrieg*, 56; Wilson, *Under the Old Flag*, 51.
49. Wilson, *Under the Old Flag*, 51; 49 *OR* 1, 405.
50. Henry, "Private Hubbard's Notes," *As They Saw Forrest*, 212–13; Wyeth, *That Devil Forrest*, 521; Wilson, *Under the Old Flag*, 51.

51. Henry, "Private Hubbard's Notes," *As They Saw Forrest*, 212–23.
52. Ibid.
53. Montgomery, *Reminiscences of a Mississippian in Peace and War*, chapter 21.
54. McMillan, *Alabama Confederate Reader*, 405; Jones, *Yankee Blitzkrieg*, 57; Fleming, *Civil War and Reconstruction in Alabama*, 72–77.
55. 49 *OR* 1, 419.
56. Ibid., 424; Wilson, *Under the Old Flag*, 42, 52; Wyeth, *That Devil Forrest*, 522.

Chapter 4

57. Andrews, *History of the Campaign of Mobile*, 260; 49 *OR* 1, 420; Jones, *Yankee Blitzkrieg*, 60.
58. Clinton, "Military Operations of General John T. Croxton," 449; Clinton, "Closing Days of the War," 8–24.
59. Wyeth, *That Devil Forrest*, 522–23; Jones, *Yankee Blitzkrieg*, 60–61; Andrews, *History of the Campaign of Mobile*, 260.
60. 49 *OR* 2, 174.
61. Jones, *Yankee Blitzkrieg*, 61–62, 145; Andrews, *History of the Campaign of Mobile*, 260–61; Clinton, "Closing Days of the War," 10.
62. 49 *OR* 1, 421; Jones, *Yankee Blitzkrieg*, 67–69, 145–46; Wyeth, *That Devil Forrest*, 523–24.
63. 49 *OR* 1, 421.
64. Clinton, "Military Operations of General John T. Croxton," 451; Jones, *Yankee Blitzkrieg*, 146–47.
65. Clinton, "Military Operations of General John T. Croxton," 452–53.
66. Ibid.; 49 *OR* 1, 421; Longacre, "To Tuscaloosa and Beyond," 114.
67. 49 *OR* 1, 421; Clinton, "Closing Days of the War," 12–13.
68. Clinton, "Military Operations of General John T. Croxton," 454–60; Jones, *Yankee Blitzkrieg*, 149.
69. Owen, *Story of Alabama*, vol. 2, 429; Anderson, "Federal Raid into Central Alabama," 25–43; Clinton, "Military Operations of General John T. Croxton," 454–55; Clinton, "Closing Days of the War," 12–14; Hoole and McArthur, *Yankee Invasion of West Alabama*, 25–29, 48–51.
70. Anderson, "Federal Raid into Central Alabama," 38–41.
71. Ibid.
72. Ibid.; Jones, *Yankee Blitzkrieg*, 150.
73. Clinton, "Closing Days of the War," 15.

74. Ibid.; Anderson, "Federal Raid into Central Alabama," 38–39; Clinton, "Military Operations of General John T. Croxton," 456–57.
75. Hoole and McArthur, *Yankee Invasion of West Alabama*, 51; Anderson, "Federal Raid into Central Alabama," 38; Clinton, "Closing Days of the War," 15–16; Clinton, "Military Operations of General John T. Croxton," 456–57.
76. Clinton, "Military Operations of General John T. Croxton," 457–58; Clinton, "Closing Days of the War," 17–19; Anderson, "Federal Raid into Central Alabama," 37; Jones, *Yankee Blitzkrieg*, 151.
77. Clinton, "Military Operations of General John T. Croxton," 458.
78. 49 *OR* 1, 422.
79. Anderson, "Federal Raid into Central Alabama"; 49 *OR* 1, 421, 426, 505.
80. 49 *OR* 1, 505–6.

Chapter 5

81. Jones, *Yankee Blitzkrieg*, 62–63; Stockham, "Alabama Iron for the Confederacy"; Owen, *Story of Alabama*, vol. 2, 655; McKenzie, "Reconstruction of the Alabama Iron Industry"; Woodward, "Alabama Iron Manufacturing"; Kvach, "Put Their Shoulder to the Wheel."
82. Wilson, *Under the Old Flag*, 52; Owen, *Story of Alabama*, vol. 2, 655; Jones, *Yankee Blitzkrieg*, 63–64; Woodward, "Alabama Iron Manufacturing," 203–7; Vandiver, "Shelby Iron Company."
83. Jones, *Yankee Blitzkrieg*, 65; Warner, *Generals in Gray*, 1.
84. Wyeth, *That Devil Forrest*, 528–29; Wilson, *Under the Old Flag*, 52–53; 49 *OR* 1, 357–58; Jones, *Yankee Blitzkrieg*, 65–66.
85. 49 *OR* 2, 1,182; Wyeth, *That Devil Forrest*, 528; Henry, *As They Saw Forrest*, 216.
86. Jones, *Yankee Blitzkrieg*, 67; Wilson, *Under the Old Flag*, 53; Wyeth, *That Devil Forrest*, 529; Chalmers, "Forrest and His Campaigns," 451–87; Taylor, *Destruction and Reconstruction*, 219.
87. Wyeth, *That Devil Forrest*, 529–30; Montgomery, *Reminiscences of a Mississippian in Peace and War*, chapter 21.
88. Wilson, *Under the Old Flag*, 53–55; 49 *OR* 2, 156.
89. 49 *OR* 1, 350–51; Jones, *Yankee Blitzkrieg*, 70; Wilson, *Under the Old Flag*, 55; Wyeth, *That Devil Forrest*, 530; Folmar, "War Comes to Central Alabama," 196. McCook's division is described here as a "partial division," since

McCook is absent, having taken one of his brigades (LaGrange's) to Centerville, under orders from Wilson, to seize and destroy the Cahaba River bridge.

90. Folmar, "War Comes to Central Alabama," 197–98. In both secondary and primary sources, Bogler's Creek also appears as "Bolger's Creek."
91. Ibid.
92. Wilkins, "In the Last Days of the Confederacy."
93. Wilson, *Under the Old Flag*, 55.
94. Wyeth, *That Devil Forrest*, 531–32.
95. Ibid.
96. Trudeau, *Out of the Storm*, 156–57; Wyeth, *That Devil Forrest*, 531–33.
97. Wilson, *Under the Old Flag*, 55.
98. Wyeth, *That Devil Forrest*, 531–33; Trudeau, *Out of the Storm*, 157.
99. Trudeau, *Out of the Storm*, 157–58.
100. Wilkins, "In the Last Days of the Confederacy," 329.
101. Wyeth, *That Devil Forrest*, 530, 534; Wilson, *Under the Old Flag*, 56.

Chapter 6

102. Brewer, *Alabama, Her History*, 208; Pierrepont, *Reuben Vaughan Kidd*, 365; Jones, *Yankee Blitzkrieg*, 79.
103. Owen, *Story of Alabama*, vol. 1, 416–18; vol. 2, 654–56; Stockham, "Alabama Iron for the Confederacy"; Massey, *Refugee Life in the Confederacy*, 87–88; Carpenter, "James D. Lynch in War and Peace."
104. Jones, *Yankee Blitzkrieg*, 75–81; Owen, *Story of Alabama*, vol. 2, 145–48.
105. Fitts, *Selma*, 57; Pierrepont, *Reuben Vaughan Kidd*, 366; Jones, *Yankee Blitzkrieg*, 79–80.
106. Landis, "Siege and Fall of Selma," 96; Fitts, *Selma*, 57; *Selma Evening Reporter*, March 28, 1865.
107. Jackson, *Story of Selma*, 214–15.
108. Davis, *Jefferson Davis*, 603; Landis, "Siege and Fall of Selma."
109. Taylor, *Destruction and Reconstruction*, 219; Trudeau, *Out of the Storm*, 160.
110. Hardy, *Selma*, 51; Jackson, *Story of Selma*, 215–16; Pierrepont, *Reuben Vaughan Kidd*, 369; Ellison, "Lewis Sydney Riggs," 49–50; Andrews, *History of the Campaign of Mobile*, 253; Wyeth, *That Devil Forrest*, 534.
111. Fitts, *Selma*, 59; Bayne, "Bayne Family," 85; Wynn, "Bankshire Rose," 1–2; Hardy, *Selma*, 52.
112. Wilson, *Under the Old Flag*, 56–57.

113. Ibid., 57; Jones, *Yankee Blitzkrieg*, 86.
114. 49 *OR* 1, 359–60, 438; Trudeau, *Out of the Storm*, 162–63.
115. 49 *OR* 1, 359–60, 438.
116. Wynn, "Bankshire Rose," 1; Montgomery, *Reminiscences of a Mississippian in Peace and War*, chapter 21.
117. Pierrepont, *Reuben Vaughan Kidd*, 368.

Chapter 7

118. Wilson, *Under the Old Flag*, 58; Gilpin, "Last Campaign," 639.
119. Montgomery, *Reminiscences of a Mississippian in Peace and War*, chapter 21.
120. Ibid.
121. Trudeau, *Out of the Storm*, 164; Wilson, *Under the Old Flag*, 58; Fitts, *Selma*, 59; 49 *OR* 1, 439.
122. 49 *OR* 1, 393; Jones, *Yankee Blitzkrieg*, 87.
123. Montgomery, *Reminiscences of a Mississippian in Peace and War*, chapter 21.
124. Trudeau, *Out of the Storm*, 164; Wyeth, *That Devil Forrest*, 535.
125. Wilson, *Under the Old Flag*, 58; Trudeau, *Out of the Storm*, 164. It's probable, though no documentation was found, that Wilson named his favorite horse "Sheridan" after the famous cavalry commander, Phil Sheridan, a man whom his biographer, Longacre, says "particularly impressed him."
126. Wilson, *Under the Old Flag*, 58–59; Wyeth, *That Devil Forrest*, 535; 49 *OR* 1, 360; Pierrepont, *Reuben Vaughan Kidd*, 371.
127. Montgomery, *Reminiscences of a Mississippian in Peace and War*, chapter 21; Johnson and Buel, *Battles and Leaders of the Civil War*, vol. 4, 760; Wynn, "Bankshire Rose," 1, 49; Pierrepont, *Reuben Vaughan Kidd*, 376.
128. Trudeau, *Out of the Storm*, 165; Pierrepont, *Reuben Vaughan Kidd*, 372–73, 376; Parsons, "Sacking of Selma."
129. Hardy, *Selma*, 51; Fitts, *Selma*, 59; Gilpin, "Last Campaign," 640.
130. Armes, *Story of Coal and Iron in Alabama*, 194.
131. Montgomery, *Reminiscences of a Mississippian in Peace and War*, chapter 21; Landis, "Siege and Fall of Selma."
132. Wilson, *Under the Old Flag*, 59; Pierrepont, *Reuben Vaughan Kidd*, 372. Several sources contend that the fires could have been extinguished or at least confined by Wilson's troops if the town's fire engines could have been located.
133. Wyeth, *That Devil Forrest*, 536.

134. 49 *OR* 1, 406; Wyeth, *That Devil Forrest*, 536–39; Jones, *Yankee Blitzkrieg*, 97; Robert Selph Henry, *"First with the Most" Forrest*, 432–33; General Viscount Wolseley, "General Viscount Wolseley on Forrest," in Henry, *As They Saw Forrest*, 35–36; John Milton Hubbard, "Private Hubbard's Notes," in Henry, *As They Saw Forrest*, 216. While versions on this incident vary, most accounts agree that Forrest was not present at the attack on the Godwin farm. The biographers of Thomas, Don Piatt and H.V. Boynton, authors of *Life of George H. Thomas*, are referred to by Wyeth, *That Devil Forrest*, 539. As to the issue of whether or not a surprise massacre took place, it's difficult to reconcile the Confederates' version of the Union firing the first shot and a desperate fight ensuing when the losses were so skewed. In other words, how could the Confederates have incurred but one loss against so many Union losses unless the attack was made without warning on sleeping men?
135. Hubbard, "Private Hubbard's Notes," in Henry, *As They Saw Forrest*, 217.

Chapter 8

136. Wilson, *Under the Old Flag*, 59–60, 42.
137. Ibid., 60; 49 *OR* 1, 351, 361.
138. Wilson, *Under the Old Flag*, 60; Jones, *Yankee Blitzkrieg*, 96. Landis, "Siege and Fall of Selma"; Fitts, *Selma*, 60; Hardy, *Selma*, 52; "The Carcasses…," quoted in Fleming, *Civil War and Reconstruction in Alabama*, 73.
139. Wilson, *Under the Old Flag*, 59–61.
140. Jones, *Yankee Blitzkrieg*, 96; McMillan, *Alabama Confederate Reader*, 416; Dallas County Heritage Book Committee, *Heritage of Dallas County, Alabama*, 71, 73; Jackson, *Some of the Boys*, 248.
141. Hardy, *Selma*, 52; Jackson, *Story of Selma*, 219; Phillips, "Reminiscences of War."
142. 49 *OR* 1, 483–84; Wilson, *Under the Old Flag*, 60.
143. Jones, *Yankee Blitzkrieg*, 98–99; Henry, *"First with the Most" Forrest*, 433–34; Wilson, *Under the Old Flag*, 61.
144. Trudeau, *Out of the Storm*, 170; Hosea, "Some Side Lights," 17–18.
145. Wilson, *Under the Old Flag*, 61; Hosea, "Some Side Lights."
146. Wilson, *Under the Old Flag*, 61; Trudeau, *Out of the Storm*, 173.
147. Wilson, *Under the Old Flag*, 62.
148. Ibid.
149. Ibid.

150. Ibid.
151. Henry, *"First with the Most" Forrest*, 434; Hosea, "Some Side Lights."
152. Jones, *Yankee Blitzkrieg*, 99–100.

Chapter 9

153. Gilpin, "Last Campaign," 645; Jones, *Yankee Blitzkrieg*, 100–101; Wilson, *Under the Old Flag*, 62; 49 *OR* 1, 351–52, 362. Some secondary accounts speculate that the Confederates were responsible for sending the floating logs and trees downstream to destroy the bridge. These accounts, however, offer no credible testimony supporting such a claim.
154. Trudeau, *Out of the Storm*, 180.
155. Wilson, *Under the Old Flag*, 63.
156. Massey, *Refugee Life in the Confederacy*, 86–88.
157. Wilson, *Under the Old Flag*, 63.
158. Ibid.; Montgomery, *Reminiscences of a Mississippian in Peace and War*, chapter 21.
159. Wilson, *Under the Old Flag*, 63.
160. 49 *OR* 1, 407; Gilpin, "Last Campaign," 647–48.
161. Gilpin, "Last Campaign," 648; Wilson, *Under the Old Flag*, 63.
162. 49 *OR* 1, 407; Jones, *Yankee Blitzkrieg*, 104–5.
163. 49 *OR* 1, 370–71; Gilpin, "Last Campaign," 648.
164. Wilson, *Under the Old Flag*, 63–64; Jones, *Yankee Blitzkrieg*, 106–7.
165. Owen, *Story of Alabama*, vol. 2, 630–32; Davis, *Jefferson Davis*, 306–7.
166. *Memphis Daily Appeal*, March 30, 1865; *Montgomery Daily Mail*, April 2, 1865; Jones, *Yankee Blitzkrieg*, 107.
167. Massey, *Refugee Life in the Confederacy*, 87–88, 166; Harwell, *Kate*, 89, 243.
168. *Montgomery Daily Mail*, April 11, 1865; Rogers and Howard, "Fall of Montgomery"; Jones, *Yankee Blitzkrieg*, 108–10.
169. Rogers and Howard, "Fall of Montgomery."
170. Catts, "Wilson's Raid and Other Recitals," 430–37.
171. Jones, "Journal of Sarah G. Follansbee," 213, 229.
172. 49 *OR* 1, 504–5; 49 *OR* 2, 1,239; *Montgomery Advertiser*, April 18, 1865; Jones, "Journal of Sarah G. Follansbee," 231; Rogers and Howard, "Fall of Montgomery."
173. Rogers and Howard, "Fall of Montgomery"; *Montgomery Daily Mail*, April 17, 1865; McMillan, *Alabama Confederate Reader*, 419; Rogers, *Confederate Home Front*, 145.

174. McMillan, *Alabama Confederate Reader*, 420: Rogers and Howard, "Fall of Montgomery"; Jones, *Yankee Blitzkrieg*, 111.
175. Jones, "Journal of Sarah G. Follansbee," 230–31.
176. *Montgomery Daily Mail*, April 17, 1865.
177. Ibid.; Rogers and Howard, "Fall of Montgomery"; Wilson, *Under the Old Flag*, 64.
178. Wilson, *Under the Old Flag*, 64; Jones, "Journal of Sarah G. Follansbee," 231.
179. Rogers and Howard, "Fall of Montgomery"; Rogers, *Confederate Home Front*, 147–48; Wilson, *Under the Old Flag*, 64; McMillan, *Alabama Confederate Reader*, 421–22; 49 *OR* 1, 407.
180. 49 *OR* 1, 433–34; Wilson, *Under the Old Flag*, 65.
181. 49 *OR* 2, 344.

Chapter 10

182. 49 *OR* 2, 345; Wilson, *Under the Old Flag*, 66; Jones, *Yankee Blitzkrieg*, 118. The city of Girard is now known as Phenix City, Alabama.
183. 49 *OR* 1, 428, 436.
184. Ibid., 436; Jones, *Yankee Blitzkrieg*, 119.
185. Wilson, *Under the Old Flag*, 65. In this account written after the war, Wilson's remark about the town being the "seat of education" was, in addition to the seminaries and schools there at the time, a reference to Tuskegee University, a historically black college founded and "made famous by Booker T. Washington" in the early 1880s.
186. Ellison, "Huntington College," 4–15.
187. Wilson, *Under the Old Flag*, 65–66.
188. Ibid.
189. Ibid., 66; Ellison, "Huntington College."
190. Wilson, *Under the Old Flag*, 66; 49 *OR* 1, 428; Jones, *Yankee Blitzkrieg*, 122.
191. 49 *OR* 1, 428, 431–32.
192. Ibid., 428; Johnson and Buel, *Battles and Leaders of the Civil War*, vol. 4, 761.
193. Warner, *Generals in Gray*, 312–13.
194. Ibid.; Slatter, "Last Battle of the War," 381.
195. 49 *OR* 1, 364, 428, 429, 432, 436.
196. Ibid.; Slatter, "Last Battle of the War," 121–25.
197. Wilson, *Under the Old Flag*, 68.

198. Ibid., 73, 76; *Columbus Sun*, April 16, 1865; Jones, *Yankee Blitzkrieg*, 132–33.
199. Wilson, *Under the Old Flag*, 66; Jones, *Yankee Blitzkrieg*, 134–35.
200. Wilson, *Under the Old Flag*, 66.
201. Ibid.
202. Ibid.
203. Wilson, *Under the Old Flag*, 66.
204. 49 *OR* 1, 480, 483; Mills, *Harvest of Barren Regrets*.
205. Captain Henricks quoted in Jones, *Yankee Blitzkrieg*, 136–37.
206. Wilson, *Under the Old Flag*, 67; Jones, *Yankee Blitzkrieg*, 137–38.
207. Brannan, "Incident of the Last Campaign," C-44–C-46.
208. Harwell, *Kate*, 272; King, *War-Time Journal of a Georgia Girl*, 146; 49 *OR* 2, 383; Wilson, *Under the Old Flag*, 68.
209. 49 *OR* 1, 365, 485–87; Wilson, *Under the Old Flag*, 68.
210. Wilson, *Under the Old Flag*, 68–69.

Chapter 11

211. Ibid., 62; 49 *OR* 2, 344.
212. Owens, "Federal Invasion of Pickens County," 93; 49 *OR* 1, 422, 426.
213. 49 *OR* 1, 422; Clinton, "Military Operations of General John T. Croxton," 461; Owens, "Federal Invasion of Pickens County," 94–97; Longacre, "To Tuscaloosa and Beyond," 116.
214. Warner, *Generals in Blue*, 104; Owens, "Federal Invasion of Pickens County," 96.
215. 49 *OR* 1, 422; 49 *OR* 2, 1,207, 1,213; Warner, *Generals in Gray*, 2–3.
216. Evans, *Confederate Military History*, 235–36.
217. Owens, "Federal Invasion of Pickens County," 99.
218. Ibid., 99–100.
219. Ibid.
220. Longacre, "To Tuscaloosa and Beyond," 116–17.
221. Jones, *Yankee Blitzkrieg*, 155; Owens, "Federal Invasion of Pickens County," 101–5; Andrews, *History of the Campaign of Mobile*, 262–63.
222. Andrews, *History of the Campaign of Mobile*, 264; Jones, *Yankee Blitzkrieg*, 156.
223. 49 *OR* 1, 422; Owens, "Federal Invasion of Pickens County," 107–12.
224. 49 *OR* 1, 426.
225. Clinton, "Military Operations of General John T. Croxton," 462; Owens, "Federal Invasion of Pickens County," 106–7.

226. Owens, "Federal Invasion of Pickens County," 107; Foote, *Civil War*, 1,026–27.
227. Jones, *Yankee Blitzkrieg*, 156–57.
228. 49 *OR* 1, 423; Longacre, "To Tuscaloosa and Beyond," 118–19.
229. 49 *OR* 1, 423; Wilson, *Under the Old Flag*, 74; Jones, *Yankee Blitzkrieg*, 157.
230. Wilson, *Under the Old Flag*, 74; Andrews, *History of the Campaign of Mobile*, 265; Warner, *Generals in Gray*, 135–36; Longacre, "To Tuscaloosa and Beyond"; 49 *OR* 1, 423.
231 Jones, *Yankee Blitzkrieg*, 158; Wilson, *Under the Old Flag*, 74.
232. 49 *OR* 1, 424; Wilson, *Under the Old Flag*, 74.

Chapter 12

233. Wilson, *Under the Old Flag*, 78.
234. Ibid., 80; Davis, *Jefferson Davis*, 636–37.
235. Davis, *Honorable Defeat*, 300–303; Davis, *Jefferson Davis*, 636–37.
236. Davis, *Honorable Defeat*, 300–303. Because Davis had mistakenly picked up his wife's cloak and had her veil over his head, the rumor soon spread that he had tried to escape in his wife's clothing, including her dress. Northern newspapers and magazines continued to report this fabrication as fact, further disgracing the Confederate president after his capture.
237. Ibid.
238. Wilson, *Under the Old Flag*, 84–85; Jones, *Yankee Blitzkrieg*, 176; Davis, *Jefferson Davis*, 637–38; Davis, *Honorable Defeat*, 306.
239. Wilson, *Under the Old Flag*, 85.
240. 49 *OR* 1, 379; Jones, *Yankee Blitzkrieg*, 180; Wilson, *Under the Old Flag*, 87–88.
241. Wyeth, *That Devil Forrest*, 540; Hurst, *Nathan Bedford Forrest*, 253–55; 49 *OR* 2, 1,263–64.
242. Simpson and Berlin, *Sherman's Civil War*, 871–72; Henry, *"First with the Most" Forrest*, 436.
243. 49 *OR* 2, 568–69.
244. Hurst, *Nathan Bedford Forrest*, 255–57; Henry, *"First with the Most" Forrest*, 437; Wyeth, *That Devil Forrest*, 540–41.
245. Wyeth, *That Devil Forrest*, 541–42; Hurst, *Nathan Bedford Forrest*, 256–61.
246. Hurst, *Nathan Bedford Forrest*, 256–58.

Analysis

247. Woodward, "Alabama Iron Manufacturing," 199–207.
248. Longacre, *From Union Stars to Top Hat*, 289.
249. Jones, *Yankee Blitzkrieg*, 187; Davis, *Jefferson Davis*, 604–39, 697.
250. Grant, *Personal Memoirs of U.S. Grant*, 621.
251. Henry, *"First with the Most" Forrest*, 19; Catton, *This Hallowed Ground*, 372; Catton, *Grant Takes Command*, 407.

Bibliography

Primary Materials

Newspapers

Columbus Sun
Memphis Daily Appeal
Montgomery Advertiser
Montgomery Daily Mail
Selma Evening Reporter
Tuscaloosa Observer

Books and Articles

Andrews, C.C. *History of the Campaign of Mobile Including the Cooperative Operations of General Wilson's Cavalry in Alabama*. New York: D. Van Nostrand, 1867.

Bayne, Elliott. "The Bayne Family." *The Heritage of Dallas County, Alabama.* Clanton, AL: Heritage Publishing Consultants Inc., 2004.

Chalmers, James R. "Forrest and His Campaigns." *Southern Historical Society Papers* 7 (October 1879).

Ellison, Aurelia Morgan. "Lewis Sydney Riggs." *The Heritage of Dallas County, Alabama.* Clanton, AL: Heritage Publishing Consultants Inc., 2004.

Gilpin, E.N. "The Last Campaign: A Cavalryman's Journal." *Journal of the United States Cavalry Association* (April 1908).

Grant, Ulysses S. *Personal Memoirs of U.S. Grant.* New York: Penguin Books, 1999.

Harwell, Richard Barksdale, ed. *Kate: The Journal of a Confederate Nurse.* Baton Rouge: Louisiana State University Press, 1959, 1987.

Henry, Robert Selph, ed. *As They Saw Forrest: Some Recollections and Comments of Contemporaries.* Jackson, TN: McCowat-Mercer Press Inc., 1956.

Hoole, William Stanley, ed., *Reconstruction in West Alabama: The Memoirs of John L. Hunnicutt.* Tuscaloosa, AL: Confederate Publishing Company Inc., 1959.

Hosea, Lewis M. "Some Side Lights on the War for the Union." *Papers Read Before the Ohio Commandery of the Military Order of the Loyal Legion of the United States.* Cleveland, Ohio, 1912.

Jackson, Joseph Orville, ed. *Some of the Boys: The Civil War Letters of Isaac Jackson, 1862–1865.* Carbondale: Illinois University Press, 1960.

Johnson, Robert U., and Clarence C. Buel, eds. *Battles and Leaders of the Civil War.* 4 vols. New York: Century, 1887. Reprint, Edison, NJ: Castle, n.d.

Jones, Virginia K., ed. "The Journal of Sarah G. Follansbee." *Alabama Historical Quarterly* 27, nos. 1 and 2 (Spring and Summer 1965).

King, Spencer Bidwell, ed. *Eliza Frances Andrews: The War-Time Journal of a Georgia Girl, 1864–1865.* Atlanta, GA: Cherokee Publishing Company, 1976.

Landis, C.E. "The Siege and Fall of Selma, Alabama." *Confederate Veteran* 31 (January 1923).

Longacre, Edward G., ed., "To Tuscaloosa and Beyond: A Union Cavalry Raider in Alabama, March—April, 1865." *Alabama Historical Quarterly* 44, nos. 1 and 2 (Spring and Summer 1982).

Montgomery, Frank Alexander. *Reminiscences of a Mississippian in Peace and War.* Cincinnati: Robert Clarke, 1901. Reprint, Middletown, DE, 2016.

Parsons, Lewis. "The Sacking of Selma." In "Raids—Wilson." Unpublished speech, Alabama Department of Archives and History, Montgomery, Alabama.

Phillips, Sarah Ellen. "Reminiscences of War and Episodes of Wilson's Raid near Selma." Unpublished manuscript, SPR7, Alabama Department of Archives and History, Montgomery, Alabama.

Simpson, Brooks D., and Berlin Jean V., eds. *Sherman's Civil War: Selected Correspondence of William T. Sherman, 1860–1865.* Chapel Hill: University of North Carolina Press, 1999.

Slatter, W.J. "Last Battle of the Civil War." *Confederate Veteran* 4, no. 1 (January 1896).

Taylor, Richard. *Destruction and Reconstruction: Personal Experiences of the Late War.* New York: D. Appleton and Company, 1879.

U.S. War Department. *The War of the Rebellion: A Compilation of the Official Records of the Union and Confederate Armies.* 129 vols. Washington, D.C.: Government Printing Office, 1880–1901.

Wilkins, J.B. "In the Last Days of the Confederacy." *Confederate Veteran* 24 (January 1916).

Wilson, James Harrison. *Under the Old Flag: Recollections of Military Operations in the War for the Union, The Spanish War, The Boxer Rebellion, Etc.* New York: D. Appleton and Company, 1912. Reprint, Memphis, TN: General Books LLC, 2012.

Wynn, O.S. "The Bankshire Rose." *The Heritage of Dallas County, Alabama.* Clanton, AL: Heritage Publishing Consultants Inc., 2004.

SECONDARY MATERIALS

Books and Articles

Anderson, James A. "The Federal Raid into Central Alabama, April, 1865." In "The Federal Invasion of Tuscaloosa, 1865." Unpublished. Printed by General Robert E. Rhodes Camp No. 262, Sons of Confederate Veterans, Tuscaloosa, Alabama.

Armes, Ethel. *The Story of Coal and Iron in Alabama.* Birmingham, AL: Chamber of Commerce, 1910.

Brannan, Peter A. "An Incident of the Last Campaign." *The History of Russell County, Alabama.* Dallas, TX: National Share Graphics Inc., 1982.

Brewer, Willis. *Alabama: Her History, Resources, War Record, and Public Men.* Spartanburg, SC: Reprint Company Publishers, 1975.

Carpenter, James A. "James D. Lynch in War and Peace." *Alabama Historical Quarterly* 20, no.1 (Spring 1958).

Castel, Albert. *Decision in the West: The Atlanta Campaign of 1864.* Lawrence: University Press of Kansas, 1992.

Catton, Bruce. *Grant Takes Command.* Boston: Little, Brown and Company, 1968.

———. *This Hallowed Ground.* Garden City, NY: Doubleday & Company, 1956.

Catts, Samuel Walker. "Wilson's Raid and Other Recitals." *Alabama Historical Quarterly* 5, no. 4 (Winter 1943).

Clanahan, James F. *The History of Pickens County, Alabama.* Carrollton, AL: Clanahan Publication, 1964.

Clinton, Thomas P. "The Closing Days of the War of Secession in Tuscaloosa." In "Federal Invasion of Tuscaloosa, 1865." Unpublished. Printed by General Robert E. Rhodes Camp No. 262, Sons of Confederate Veterans, Tuscaloosa, Alabama.

———. "The Military Operations of General John T. Croxton in West Alabama, 1865." *Transactions of the Alabama Historical Society, 1899–1903.* Vol. 4. 1904. Montgomery, AL, 1904.

Connelly, Thomas L. *Autumn of Glory: The Army of Tennessee, 1862–1865.* Baton Rouge: Louisiana State University Press, 1972.

Dallas County Heritage Book Committee, comp. *The Heritage of Dallas County, Alabama.* Clanton, AL: Heritage Publishing Consultants Inc., 2004.

Davis, William C. *An Honorable Defeat: The Last Days of the Confederate Government.* San Diego, CA: Harcourt Inc., 2001.

———. *Jefferson Davis: The Man and His Hour.* Baton Rouge: Louisiana State University Press, 1991.

Ellison, Rhoda Coleman. "Huntington College." *Alabama Review* 7, no.1 (January 1954).

Evans, Clement, ed. *Confederate Military History Extended Addition.* 17 vols. Wilmington, NC: Bradford Publishing Company, 1899.

Faust, Drew Gilpin. *This Republic of Suffering: Death and the American Civil War.* New York: Vintage Books, 2008.

Fitts, Alston, III. *Selma: Queen City of the Black Belt.* Selma, AL: Clairmont Press, 1989.

Fleming, Walter. *Civil War and Reconstruction in Alabama.* New York: Peter Smith, 1949.

Folmar, John Kent. "The War Comes to Central Alabama: Ebenezer Church, April 1, 1865." *Alabama Historical Quarterly* 26, no. 2 (Summer 1964).

Foote, Shelby. *The Civil War, a Narrative: Red River to Appomattox.* New York: Random House, 1974.

Groom, Winston. *Shrouds of Glory—From Atlanta to Nashville: The Last Great Campaign of the Civil War.* New York: Atlantic Monthly Press, 1995.

Hardy, John. *Selma: Her Institutions and Her Men.* Selma, AL: Times Book and Jobs Office, 1879.

Henry, Robert Selph. *"First with the Most" Forrest.* Indianapolis, IN: Bobbs-Merrill Company, 1944. Reprint, Greenwood Press Publishers, 1974.

Hoole, William Stanley, and Elizabeth Hoole McArthur. *The Yankee Invasion of West Alabama, March–April, 1865.* Tuscaloosa, AL: Confederate Publishing Company, n.d.

Horn, Stanley F. *The Army of Tennessee.* Norman: University of Oklahoma Press, 1952.

Hurst, Jack. *Nathan Bedford Forrest: A Biography.* New York: Alfred A. Knopf, 1993.

Jackson, Walter M. *The Story of Selma.* Birmingham, AL: Birmingham Printing Company, 1954.

Jones, James Pickett. *Yankee Blitzkrieg: Wilson's Raid through Alabama and Georgia.* Athens: University of Georgia Press, 1976.

King, Spencer Bidwell, Jr., ed. *The War-Time Journal of a Georgia Girl, 1864–1865.* Atlanta, GA: Cherokee Publishing Company, 1976.

Kvach, John F. "Put Their Shoulder to the Wheel." *Alabama Heritage*, no. 120 (Spring 2016).

Longacre, Edward G. *From Union Stars to Top Hat: A Biography of the Extraordinary General James Harrison Wilson.* Harrisburg, PA: Stackpole Books, 1972.

Massey, Mary Elizabeth. *Refugee Life in the Confederacy.* Baton Rouge: Louisiana State University Press, 1964.

McKenzie, Robert H. "Reconstruction of the Alabama Iron Industry." *Alabama Review* 25, no. 3 (July 1972).

McMillan, Malcolm C. *The Alabama Confederate Reader.* Tuscaloosa: University of Alabama Press, 1963.

Mills, Charles K. *Harvest of Barren Regrets: The Army Career of Frederick William Benteen, 1834–1898.* Glendale, CA: Arthur H. Clark Company, 1985.

O'Brien, Sean Michael. *Mobile, 1865: Last Stand for the Confederacy.* Westport, CT: Praeger Publishers, 2001.

Owen, Marie Bankhead. *The Story of Alabama: A History of the State.* 5 vols. New York: Lewis Historical Publishing, 1949.

Owens, Scott W. "The Federal Invasion of Pickens County, April 5–7, 1865: Croxton's Sipsey River Campaign." *Alabama Review* 62, no. 2 (Spring 2009).

Pierrepont, Alice V.D. *Reuben Vaughan Kidd, Soldier of the Confederacy.* Petersburg, VA: Violet Bank, 1947.

Rogers, William Warren, and Howard Milo Barrett Jr. "The Fall of Montgomery." *Montgomery Advertiser.* March 16, 1959.

Rogers, William Warren, Jr. *Confederate Home Front: Montgomery During the Civil War.* Tuscaloosa: University of Alabama Press, 1999.

Still, William. *Iron Afloat.* Nashville, TN: Vanderbilt University Press, 1971.

Stockham, Robert J. "Alabama Iron for the Confederacy: The Selma Works." *Alabama Review* 21, no. 3 (July 1968).

Trudeau, Noah Andre. *Out of the Storm: The End of the Civil War, April–June 1865.* Boston: Little, Brown and Company, 1994.

Vandiver, Frank E. "The Shelby Iron Company in the Civil War: A Study of a Confederate Industry." *Alabama Review* 1, no. 1 (January 1948).

Warner, Ezra J. *Generals in Blue: Lives of the Union Commanders.* Baton Rouge: Louisiana State University Press, 1964.

———. *Generals in Gray: Lives of the Confederate Commanders.* Baton Rouge: Louisiana State University Press, 1959.

Wiley, Bell Irvin. *The Life of Johnny Reb: The Common Soldier of the Confederacy.* Baton Rouge: Louisiana State University Press, 1943.

Wills, Brian Steel. "The Confederate Sun Sets on Selma." In *The Yellowhammer War: The Civil War and Reconstruction in Alabama.* Edited by Kenneth W. Noe. Tuscaloosa: University of Alabama Press, 2013.

Woodward, Joseph H. "Alabama Iron Manufacturing, 1860–1865." *Alabama Review* 7, no. 3 (July 1954).

Wyeth, John Allen. *That Devil Forrest: Life of General Nathan Bedford Forrest.* Baton Rouge: Louisiana State University Press, 1959.

Index

L

M

N

O

P

R

S

T

U

V

W

Y

About the Author

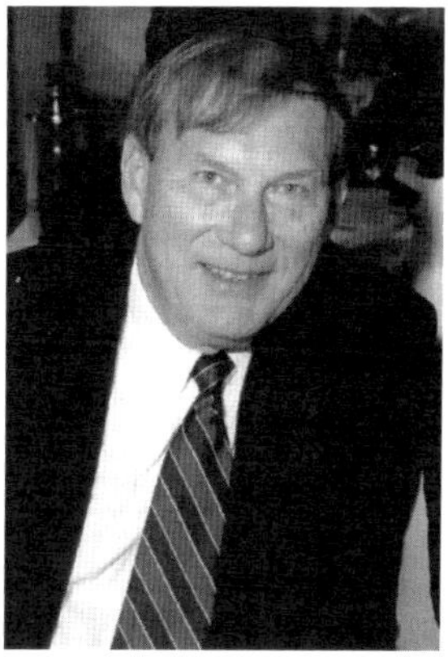

Russell W. Blount Jr. is a retired senior vice-president of Surety Land Title Inc. He is the author of four books on the American Civil War and has taught history at the high school level. An Alabama native, Blount is involved with a number of historical organizations, such as the Historic Mobile Preservation Society, the Sons of Confederate Veterans and the Civil War Trust. He is a frequent speaker at Civil War roundtables, battlefield parks, museums and other historical forums.